What people a

A Bulletproof Ground Sloth: On the Hunt in Brazil

Pat Spain is that rare thing; a rationalist who still embraces the possible and knows that there are more things in heaven and earth than are dreamt of. A grown-up who has lost none of the childhood wonder and curiosity that makes the world magical. A scientist who keeps an open mind and rejoices in the fact that absence of proof is not proof of absence. There is nobody I'd want to travel with more to explore the wild side of our literally extraordinary planet. Buckle up and prepare for adventures.
Harry Marshall, Chairman and Co-Founder of Icon Films

For many years I have been a raving fan of Pat's work and proudly boast *Beast Hunter* as my all-time favorite crypto-history series. I've watched his Bullet Ant ritual many times but to read and learn about the entire journey was absolutely fascinating. Clutched to the edge of my seat, I found myself glued to each and every word. As someone who has felt the burning wrath of an intentional Bullet Ant sting, I can attest to the insane level of pain that comes from just a single dose of venom, but to wear the gloves and take an onslaught of stings is a level of bravery that deserves medals. Pat truly defines what it means to be an adventurer and in the spirit of the Sateré-Mawé tribe what it means to be... a hunter!
Coyote Peterson, Host of Brave Wilderness

Enrapturing and brilliant. Pat Spain sweeps us along on true adventures in the biological world that have us laughing, crying, and shivering all at the same time. His brilliantly described first-hand participation in the Sateré-Mawé manhood ritual involving dozens of bullet ant stings, a feat beyond even the most lion-hearted of Westerners, have us hallucinating along with him as the pain reaches a crescendo... and then beyond. A book not to be missed.

Justin O. Schmidt, author of *The Sting of the Wild*

A true modern-day explorer, Pat Spain has produced an exciting and informative account of his adventures that brings the readers along for the ride. That is probably as close as most readers would feel comfortable with!

Cliff Barackman, host of Finding Bigfoot and co-owner of the North American Bigfoot Center

A Bulletproof Ground Sloth: On the Hunt in Brazil

or How I Lost My Mind, Was Dyed Blue, and Accidentally Learned How to Smuggle Weapons

A Bulletproof Ground Sloth: On the Hunt in Brazil

or How I Lost My Mind, Was Dyed Blue, and Accidentally Learned How to Smuggle Weapons

Pat Spain

6TH
BOOKS

Winchester, UK
Washington, USA

JOHN HUNT PUBLISHING

First published by Sixth Books, 2023
Sixth Books is an imprint of John Hunt Publishing Ltd., No. 3 East St., Alresford,
Hampshire SO24 9EE, UK
office@jhpbooks.com
www.johnhuntpublishing.com
www.6th-books.com

For distributor details and how to order please visit the 'Ordering' section on our website.

Text copyright: Pat Spain 2021

ISBN: 978 1 78904 652 6
978 1 78904 653 3 (ebook)
Library of Congress Control Number: 2021942473

A CIP catalogue record for this book is available from the British Library.

Design: Stuart Davies

UK: Printed and bound by CPI Group (UK) Ltd, Croydon, CR0 4YY
Printed in North America by CPI GPS partners

We operate a distinctive and ethical publishing philosophy in
all areas of our business, from our global network of authors to
production and worldwide distribution.

Contents

This book is for my kids, Luna Caulfield and Wallace Charles. This world is an amazing and wonderful place, and there are many refrigerators in your future that will need magnets.

Introduction

Some of you may know me as the "(almost) King of the Jungle," "Legend Hunter," "that animal guy," "Beast Hunter" or "that guy who had cancer and catches snakes." Probably not, though. Despite having a couple of dozen hours of international TV series to my name, and giving hundreds of talks and presentations, I don't really get recognized very often – unless we're talking about college kids in Guwahati India, middle-aged men in the US, or pre-teen Indonesian girls. My key demographics, it turns out. I struggle to name anything those groups have in common, besides me.

I left my home in Upstate New York at 16 to live in a barn in southern Maine for a marine biology internship, and I haven't stopped exploring since. My passion for wildlife led me to create my own YouTube-based wildlife series in 2004 and has landed me spots on Animal Planet, Nat Geo, Nat Geo Wild, Travel Channel, SyFy, BBC and more. Half of the TV shows I've made have never seen the light of day, but they were all an adventure and there isn't a single one I wouldn't do again if given the chance. Besides TV, I work full time in biotech, which is its own sort of adventure – albeit one where drinking the water is generally safer. I've been bitten and stung by just about everything you can think of – from rattlesnakes and black bears to bullet ants and a rabid raccoon – and I've lost count of the number of countries I've been to.

I've had the opportunity to travel the world, interacting with some of the strangest and rarest animals, while having the honor of living with indigenous peoples in some of the most remote locations – participating in their rituals, eating traditional meals, and massively embarrassing myself while always trying to remain respectful. I am a perpetual fish out of water, even in my home state of Massachusetts. This book is part of the "On the Hunt" series, in which I get to tell some of my favorite stories from those travels.

This particular book is about my time in Brazil searching for the truth behind the mythical creature the Mapinguari with my friends, making an episode of the National Geographic Channel series *Beast Hunter* – also called *Beast Man* in the UK, *Breast Hunter* by my wife, and *Beast Master* by almost everyone who meets me for the first time and tells me they enjoyed the series.

Brazil is incredible – the people, the food, the drinks, the Amazon, the forest, the wildlife. It was my favorite shoot of the series, and one that changed my life forever. Please take the attempts at humor in the following pages for what they are and know that I mean no disrespect. I hope you enjoy this book. If you do, please pick up the others in this series. If you don't, I'll probably hear about why on social media. Either way, thanks for reading!

A disclaimer

My dog Daisy was the best. She loved hanging out in the backyard with my sister, Sarah, and me when we were playing hide-and-go-seek, catching bugs, or looking for arrow heads on the trails behind our house in Upstate NY. She would wait patiently at the base of any tree we climbed and chase away our neighbor's super scary dog (he ate a kitten once). She would also stand guard while I waited for the spider to crawl out of a crack in our chipped blue bulkhead cellar doors. It was huge, with green-metallic colored fur and red eyes, and Daisy would growl if I put my hand too close to it. She was a white poodle mix with poofy fur and perpetually muddy feet. Also, Daisy could fly, sometimes wore a cape, and would occasionally speak with a Southern drawl.

I don't have schizophrenia and Daisy was not an imaginary friend – but she also didn't really exist. Despite never owning a dog as a child, I have honest, distinct memories of Daisy.

Memories that go well beyond the stories my mom used to tell my sister and me about Daisy saving us from one tragedy or another. I also have detailed memories of being terrified, like heart-racing, nearly in tears of fear the time Cookie Monster stole our shoes while we were wading in the creek catching crayfish and pollywogs. He would only give them back when we had the Count (who smelled like toothpaste) help us negotiate how many cookies it would take for each shoe, shoelace, and sock. Daisy ran back and forth from our house bringing with her a ransom of the ever-increasing number of chocolate chip cookies that my mom had left out to cool. The monster (I think people forget he is a monster by definition) kept finding loopholes in our deals, and the tension was getting higher and higher as the water rose in the creek. Cookie Monster smelled like BO and his eyes rolled around like a crazy person's. He was unstable. In the end, Daisy came through, as she always did.

Mom would start these stories "When you were both very small, we had a wonderful dog named Daisy," and they quickly took on a life of their own. They eventually made their way into our collective consciousness as real events, complete with details not included in the original stories which must have been added by Sarah and me. It was years later, during some holiday involving drinking (see "every holiday"), that we started reminiscing about childhood memories and one of us asked: "Did we really have a dog when we were little? I kind of feel like we did, but I also can't picture us having a dog with all of the other animals we had. Daisy, maybe?" It wasn't until then that we realized these were, in fact, fictitious stories our mom had made up to keep us entertained on rainy days in our old house. Stories that drew on real events (being terrorized by a neighbor's dog, getting stuck in a creek, finding snakes, spiders, and arrowheads, etc.), with Daisy taking the place of our mother as the heroine.

I guess what I mean by this is, all of the stories in this book are exactly how I remember them, but I honestly remember having a flying southern-belle dog and interacting with Muppets. Take that how you want. I had a great childhood.

Oh, also - All views expressed are my own and do not reflect those of National Geographic, The National Geographic Channel, Icon Films, John Hunt Publishing, or any other person or organization mentioned (or not mentioned) in this book.

Chapter 1

The 24-hour ant

"It's the worst thing you can ever experience, more pain than you can imagine. You might think you know what pain is, but you don't. Think about the most terrible pain you've ever been in, pain so bad it makes you vomit and blacks out everything else in the world. Really think about it, remember it, try to feel it again now, remember the anguish, the crushing mental belief that it will never end, and know that the pain you are remembering, the worst you've *ever* experienced, that pain can't even touch what you will feel tomorrow, and the next day, and maybe even the next."

Holy shit, our boat driver got *intense* when he found out I was going to do the Tucandeira.

"So... you've done it?" I asked, more than a little shakily.

"Yeah, I've done it, and you'll be able to do it too. But it will be anguish, pure terror." He was laying it on pretty thick, but I admit I was sweating. "You didn't eat any meat today, did you? Or any fish?"

"No, I don't think so. Is it bad if I did? I can't really remember." My mind was really fuzzy, and I was getting confused. Why had he jumped from his intense speech about the ceremony to asking about my diet? "Wait, you did the Tucandeira twenty times?" I asked, still a little thrown.

He gave a huge exaggerated belly laugh, like, leaning over and slapping his legs "No, no, no, no, no, Gah hah hahhahah!" More guttural laughs. "*HELL* no. I did it once, then I said 'I can drive a boat! I don't need to be a hunter!'"

It was just past sunset, and the reality of what I had volunteered to do weeks before in Bristol was finally hitting me.

"You know, Pat," Harry said. "Oliver Heaviside was correct when he said 'In order to know soup, it is not necessary to climb into the pot and be boiled.'"

"Too right," agreed Laura. "This *doesn't* sound like a very good idea. And besides, I don't think Health and Safety will be too keen on it. Anna, please talk some sense into your partner, and I'll work on mine."

Anna and I were having dinner with Harry and Laura Marshall, the heads of the best natural-history production company in the world, Icon Films at Bristol's Riverstation Bar and Kitchen – the former workplace of Long Tall Alex, associate producer extraordinaire and giant (at 6'10" he actually is a giant, legally, in the UK), and where he first met the Marshalls and convinced them to hire him. Harry and I were working on a different sort of convincing that night. We were discussing bullet ants, and an idea I'd had a few months before that was looking more and more like a possibility.

I would be heading to the remote Amazon rainforest to host an episode of *Beast Hunter* – a TV series on The National Geographic Channel– searching for the truth behind the legend of the mythical Mapinguari. It would require getting a reclusive tribe of indigenous people, the Sateré-Mawé, to trust me enough to tell their true legends – only shared with other members of the tribe. And I'd only have a few days to earn that trust. The ants seemed like – and pardon the dad joke here – a "silver bullet" for my problem.

While Harry's words were cautionary, he grinned as he spoke, and fiddled with his cufflinks – each depicting a portion of the famous Woman of Willendorf, a Paleolithic statue of a very buxom nude woman believed to represent fertility and ideal beauty. At a glance, the cufflinks appeared to be breasts and a vulva. Harry loved them for all the *right* reasons, but also enjoyed wearing them in extremely conservative nations with views on women that Harry – with three amazing, independent, beautiful, and strong daughters – just couldn't abide.

Harry was dressed, as usual, like an eclectic 1930s Londoner with a splash of color added in the form of a Chihuly-esque swirl pattern on the inside of his perfectly tailored tweed suit jacket. Laura looked stunning in a black-and-white 1950s style evening gown with a scarf, whose acquisition story was more interesting than anything discussed at any dinner party most people have ever attended. Anna was gorgeous in skinny jeans, an asymmetrical top and a scarf we had picked up in Paris the week before, and I was the odd one out in blue and white gingham shorts and a gray Penguin polo – the fanciest clothes I had brought, or rather the fanciest clothes I owned. The more time I've spent with Harry, the more I've found myself dressing like him, and my collection of "smart" clothes has grown significantly in the interim years. We now even have a matching pair of shoes – Harry's in pink and black, mine in brown and blue.

I knew Harry was saying his cautionary piece, but was also as excited about the prospect of getting the bullet-ant ceremony, Tucandeira, on film as I was about doing it. Laura was agreeing with his caution, but I think could sense where Harry really stood, so took a different tact and implored Anna to join a united front with her against this madness. It did not take much convincing.

One of the many things I love about Anna (who is now my wife and at the time was my girlfriend of 10 years) is her encouragement of my insanity. When I tell some people about the more random things I do, their first question is "Anna lets you do that?" This is such a bizarre and foreign concept to both of us. We're adults, we don't *let* each other do anything. Anna never gets jealous, angry, or overprotective when it comes to my adventures. She'll sometimes make a statement like, "If you die, I'm going to be so pissed at you," or "If you permanently injure yourself climbing that stupid mountain, don't expect any sympathy." After a rattlesnake bit me, our phone conversation went like this:

"Heeeeeeeeeey."

"Why are you calling and acting weird? What's wrong?"

"Um, don't freak out. It's not a big deal, but I just got bitten by a neotropical rattlesnake."

"You're such an asshole. Why did you pick that stupid thing up?"

"It *was* stupid. I should have used the right equipment. I was free-handling it to get a good shot."

"For a really smart guy you are *so* dumb sometimes. What hospital are you in?"

"Well, I'm not at a hospital. I'm just waiting it out. I'm 99% sure it was a dry bite."

"Seriously, what is wrong with you? Go to the fucking hospital right now. I have to call your mom, don't I?"

When I told her I was driving cross-country with a buddy of mine, his girlfriend, and one of her friends, Anna never asked anything that a girlfriend in a romcom (and far too many real women) would ask, like: "Is she pretty? Are you all camping together? How often will you be able to call and check in?" That isn't her style. We trust each other. She just said: "Have fun and buy me something cool!" Anna is amazing and, like I said, supportive of my insanity.

We met in 1999 at Suffolk University in Boston, Massachusetts, when she was a freshman and I was a sophomore. I will never forget the first time I saw her, as it was the only time in my life I have been left literally speechless by a woman I've never spoken to. She was in a dress on her way out for the night, and I was in some dirty army pants and an old Ramones T-shirt hanging out in the cafeteria. I pretended to study the over-head menu for the entire duration she was in line and made awkward eye contact a few times, but was physically unable to speak. She was probably (rightfully) weirded out by me. She made her exit, I regained my ability to function, and I told my friends that the most attractive woman I'd ever seen had just walked out of the room.

I figured out who she was a few weeks later when it turned out that I'd be the Teaching Assistant in her intro to chem lab. I spent the next few years getting to know her – teaching a couple of her labs, assisting the teacher in others, hanging out occasionally as friends, selling her my old books. Any excuse to talk to her. I literally wrote things down to say to her the night before our labs together, then lost my nerve and just talked about the subject matter at hand, or her trip to Vietnam when she was 14 (my go-to "hey, I know a fact about you!" bullshit discussion). I sat awkwardly on my lab stool flicking my gloves against my thumb to make them "pop" and stared off in space, because I'm super cool like that. I finally got the courage to ask her out on a date at the start of my senior year. She had transferred to a different university in Boston and we were both single, and to my amazement she said yes. Our first date was at the New England Aquarium, where I worked at the time – which is the most Pat Spain thing to do, ever – and it was closed – which is actually *the* most Pat Spain thing to do, ever. We then went to a nice Italian restaurant, and when I tried being classy and asked if we should order some wine; she looked really nervous, and said, "Ummmm... I better not."

To which I replied: "Oh, I just thought wine might be nice. I'm not trying to get you drunk and take advantage of you or anything." Those words actually left my mouth.

She just said: "I mean, I'm only 20..." For those of you not in the States, the drinking age here is 21, and Anna was only trying to avoid an awkward situation of not being able to produce valid ID to get a drink, so of course, I created a *much* more awkward situation. She married me. I still don't know how or why.

Anna is 5'3" and fiercer and more loyal than anyone you could meet. She's first-generation Vietnamese and grew up in Lowell Massachusetts, former Crack Capital of America,

9

which, if she's been drinking, she will usually tell you in the form of a shouted "I'm from LOWELL" and an implied "Don't fuck with me or my family" – sometimes it's not "implied" so much as "implicitly stated." She's amazing in every way – an amazing mom, funny, kind, and super-smart (she destroyed me in organic and all other chem classes, overall GPA, Grade Point Average, and, you know, life). She also makes smart decisions, so her thoughts on bullet ants were appreciated.

When I mentioned the bullet ants a couple of weeks before that night at dinner with the Marshalls and started talking her through the process, the ritual, and the animals themselves – it was the first time she'd ever questioned one of my outlandish sounding ideas. She wasn't being at all controlling, just expressing concern. She knew enough about bullet ants to be wary of them. We had seen them in Costa Rica while filming *Nature Calls*, my web-based nature series. She'd even helped me avoid being stung by one late at night when collecting frogs and snakes in some old-growth rainforest near the small town of Guayacán de Siquirres. I leaned against a tree, putting my hand next to a giant cockroach to show a size comparison and turned towards the camera to talk about it, when Anna ran into frame and slapped my hand. I asked her what she was doing and why she had ruined the shot, and she pointed about two inches from where my hand had been. Three bullet ants were headed my way, fast, along the trunk.

"Pay attention!" Anna said. "You need to look where you put your hands in the jungle. Remember, *you* lectured all of *us* about that." She was right, of course.

"Pat, I'm really not sure this is a good idea. People die doing this. Once it starts, you have no control over the outcome. You know I'm always up for anything, but this? This seems like pushing it."

We talked about it a lot. In the end, she just asked me to play it by ear and trust myself. She asked me to do an internal check on the day of the ceremony, and if I had an off-feeling about it, if I got a bad vibe or something didn't seem right, to please not do it. Her concern gave me more pause than anything I'd read, or any caution from anyone involved in the production. I, of course, had not told my mom anything about it beforehand. I told my sister, who already thought I was insane, and who just shook her head and said, "Mom will lose her mind if you tell her."

At dinner that night in Bristol, Anna readily agreed with Laura. "I told him I thought it was ridiculous," she said. "There must be other ways to get the tribe to trust you." Laura and Anna seemed to be feeding each other's growing insecurities about the situation and validating every fear the other had. They traded terrifying comments.

"People die from one sting; you'll be getting hundreds."

"Even with a doctor present, there isn't much they can do."

"Andie [another of my favorite people in the world, and director of production at Icon] was stung in the late eighties, and she can still recall without hesitation the exact spot, and nearly breaks down just talking about it. And that was *one* sting."

"You have no idea what your reaction will be."

"You might actually go crazy from the pain – it's so intense that you can lose yourself in it."

"Why do you want to do this? People will think it's just a cheap publicity stunt."

Everything she and Anna were saying was true, and made a lot of sense. It seemed Harry and I were fighting a losing battle over a topic we weren't completely convinced of ourselves. I could tell Harry was struggling with it. He didn't want to pressure me into doing anything, but I could see in his eyes how amazing he thought it would be if I went through with it. And the entire thing had been my idea, after all.

During a production meeting with the Icon team a couple of months earlier, I hesitantly suggested my participation in the ritual. It was something I'd given a lot of thought to, but on that day said it like I was half-joking, or had just thought of it. I wanted to gauge the reaction of the room. This show provided so many opportunities, so many things I would never have been able to do on my own, I thought I'd keep adding to the list.

"If I need to get in with them [the Sateré-Mawé tribe] quickly, maybe I should do the bullet ant ritual," I said with a grin.

The conference room went silent. Harry stared at me, Barny (series producer) stopped drinking his coffee, Lady Laura (Not Marshall – our associate producer Laura) spluttered "No, absolutely not. Do you have any idea what it's like?" Ben (producer), seemingly the only other person who was into the idea, grinned and quietly said, "brilliant." A couple of years before, Steve Backshall, the famous BBC presenter and host of *Venom Hunter*, *Deadly 60*, and other excellent wildlife series, had become the first Westerner to document their participation in the ritual. His account of the bullet ants was well known in the Icon offices. In 2008, Steve wrote an excellent article about his experience for *The Sunday Times* titled "Bitten by the Amazon". It's well worth the read in it's entirety.

He describes how, after receiving several hundred stings, he begins crying, convulsing and nearly passing out from the pain. Then he says: "If there'd been a machete to hand, I'd have chopped off my arms to escape the pain" (Steve Backshall, *The Sunday Times*, "Bitten by the Amazon", 2008).

That line is worth repeating. "If there'd been a machete to hand, I'd have chopped off my arms to escape the pain." That statement stuck with me, and everyone else in the room. This was taboo – presenters did not do this ritual. Bruce Parry, host of the world-renowned *Going Tribal* TV series, imbibed every narcotic cocktail presented to him, had various parts of his body pierced and probed, became violently ill countless times, tripped his face off, and even underwent penis-inversion at the hands of numerous tribes over the three-season run of the show, but had drawn the line at bullet ants, allegedly calling it "absolutely mental." Ruud Kleinpaste, world-renowned entomologist and host of the TV series *Buggin' with Ruud* (in my opinion, one of the best and most underrated wildlife shows), has been stung and bitten by nearly every insect in the world. He received one sting from a bullet ant and broke down in tears, lost the ability to speak for hours, and claimed it was the worst, most intense and terrifying pain he had ever experienced. Steve-O and Chris Pontius from MTV's *Jackass* and *Wild Boyz* attracted the attention of great white sharks while dressed as seals, used a ham to play keep-away with a pack of hyenas, and dressed as zebras outside a lion's den, but when it came to the bullet ants, they received about five stings each before quitting, taking a huge amount of pain killers, and getting rushed to the hospital. They say that it was the dumbest, most painful, and terrifying thing they have ever done. Let *that* sink in for a minute. Steve-O – the guy who made himself shark bait by putting a hook through his chest and lip and got dragged behind a boat in shark-infested water, had an alligator snapping turtle, the animal with the strongest bite in the world, latch onto his ass, regularly stapled his genitals to his leg each night for the better part of a decade, and allowed himself to be chained inside a full-to-the-brim chemical toilet as it was inverted and shaken like a fecal-cocktail by an industrial crane, completely coating him in human excrement – said the bullet ant ceremony was the dumbest thing he had ever done, and he didn't even come close to doing the full ritual.

The full ritual would involve venturing deep into the jungle with the tribe to collect hundreds of *Paraponera clavata*, bullet ants. At over an inch long (not including the length of the jaws and stinger), the bullet ant is the second largest ant species in the world, but has the distinction of having *the* worst sting of any insect. The Schmidt Pain Index, a scale that measures the pain caused by the sting of any hymenoptera (ants, bees, wasps, etc.), describes the sting of a bullet ant as: "Pure, intense, brilliant pain. Like fire-walking over flaming charcoal with a three-inch rusty nail in your heel."

The ant derives its name from its being roughly the size of a bullet, and because if you are unfortunate enough to get stung by one, it feels like you've been shot. They are also known as fever ants, Tucandeira ants, and *Hormiga veinticuatro* – the 24-hour ant – because that gun-shot-like pain lasts a solid 24 hours. The pain is said to build and build and build beyond the point where you believe your body can possibly handle it, beyond the point where you feel "nothing can possibly hurt more than this," and then it does. It builds for five hours then peaks, then stays there for 19 hours before slowly dissipating. The residual effects of phantom pain, numbness, and muscle aches can last months. Luckily, people rarely get stung, unless you belong to the Sateré-Mawé tribe, or you have to gain their trust quickly.

Just collecting the beasts is a dangerous proposition. Heading out into the deep forest, drumming on a mound of bullet ants, and trying to gather the angry little buggers into a bamboo tube before they sting you is generally not considered a good idea. But, as an initiate, it's what you need to do. Knowing you're going to be stung is one thing, but getting stung when you don't expect it can send your body into shock and kill you. Once you've collected dozens and dozens of the killer insects, you knock them out with a narcotic cocktail and weave the unconscious bastards into gloves made of raffia leaves, stingers facing in. The ants wake up about an hour later, hungover and pissed off. One by one, the initiates have the gloves placed on their hands by a tribal elder, receiving hundreds of stings, and they must not yell or cry out in any way. If they do, the ritual ends and it doesn't count. Then they have to dance as an elder of the tribe sings for five minutes. These are five of the longest minutes of their life, because the hundreds of bullet ants in the gloves are now stinging them dozens of times each, injecting venom into the sensitive flesh of their hands.

And that is what I had just suggested I do to gain the trust of the tribe quickly. That's why everyone at the production meeting was looking at me like I was crazy, and why Harry and I changed the subject at dinner, sensing imminent defeat. Harry gave us an out by saying: "Well, it's not worth discussing until Health and Safety has had their say. I for one feel like mutton. How about you darling?" He glanced lovingly at Laura, who was inspecting the menu, eyebrows raised, attempting not to make eye contact with him, then to me, and gave me a wordless "how do *you* think that went?" raised eyebrow. I did not think it had gone well.

We had an incredible dinner and let the topic drop. After, when we were alone in Harry and Laura's guest bedroom, Anna asked again, "Do you think you'll do it?"

I could tell she was nervous. She was only in England for a few days and I wanted to set her mind at ease, but I would never lie to her. "I honestly don't know, but I promise I'll be smart about it if I do."

"That's all I ask," she said, and didn't bring it up again.

The day after Anna flew home, Ben, Sol (associate producer and translator), and I started researching the potential reactions to the ritual in depth. At first, it looked like 30 stings could kill a 175-pound guy; then a bullet ant expert gave us a revised estimate of 1500 stings. Sol even reached out to Dr. Justin "King of Sting" Schmidt, author of the Schmidt Pain Index, and received some assurance that I was unlikely to die. His words were:

My personal worries would be Pat's emotional strength and abilities, not really the medical aspects. The lethality of the venom for a normal healthy person would be several hundred stings or more, and there are no chronic or residual effects of sublethal envenomation other than the possibility of several days of pain.

There were those "several hundred" stings, popping up again as a lethal dose. How many hundred, exactly? This became a hot topic of debate. It was finally settled by Steve Backshall and his crew, who confirmed that Steve received over two times the number of stings of most initiates and, while his entire body did go into spasm, he didn't suffer any long-term effects. There could be no guarantees that I would be mentally okay, but I felt as confident as possible that this wouldn't kill me.

I've recently re-connected with Justin who published a paper in 2019 titled "Pain and Lethality Induced by Insect Stings" which details the number of stings of representative Hymenoptera based on calculations that are predicted (based on mice data) to deliver a deadly sting to a 70-kg (approx. 155 pound) person. For bullet ants, the magic number is 245.

I'm very glad we didn't know that number before we filmed, because I don't think there is any way I would have been given the greenlight to do this. As it was, even with our research, health and safety at Icon was totally against it. After I agreed to sign a million forms – essentially stating over and over that I was not being coerced, was volunteering to do this of my own free will, and wouldn't sue or hold anyone liable if I suffered a debilitating injury or died – they agreed, with some conditions. We had to have a trauma doctor on site and a medical evacuation helicopter ready to airlift me to the nearest hospital. I would also be required to do a "tester sting" at least 40 minutes before the full ritual. This would show the doctor whether I was allergic to the venom, and a potential anaphylactic reaction to one sting would be less severe than the full ritual flooding my system with the venom.

I signed the forms under the disapproving gaze of Laura

Marshall, who was still completely against the idea. Harry then urged us to write the episode with two scenarios – one where I participated in the ritual, and one where I only watched. He stressed again and again that I should back out at any point if I needed or wanted to. I started to think he was more nervous about it than me, which made me slightly terrified.

We set off for Brazil a few weeks later, and after a couple of days in Manaus and four more heading down the Amazon towards the Sateré-Mawé's land, I found myself in a hammock on the houseboat we'd call home for the next two weeks, anchored just outside of their village, the night before the ceremony was to take place. I was replaying the conversation I'd had with our captain a couple of hours before – where he laughed hysterically, real belly laughs, when I'd asked if he'd done the ceremony twenty times. Once was enough to completely change the path his life had been on – and I really thought I could handle this?

A mental dialogue started: Oh my God, I'm actually going to do this. Maybe I shouldn't do it, I told Anna I probably wouldn't do it, "I don't even know if the tribe will go for it, but if I don't do it, I don't know if they'll like me." I can remember saying that, out loud, but the "tribe" seemed a very conceptual notion when we were sitting in our apartment outside Boston. I'd lived with a few tribes before this trip, after all – nomadic herders in Mongolia, two Aka Pygmy tribes in West Africa, and others. The Baka in Cameroon loved me! I let millipedes crawl on my face and scared the little kids. They all laughed and hugged me. But this was the Sateré-Mawé tribe, who were very different than any of the other groups I'd visited. We were about four days downriver from Manaus but the Hotel Tropical felt as far away as vacation does by the end of your first day back to work.

The village of the Sateré-Mawé was on the edge of unexplored land and surrounded by "un-contacted tribes" – tribes that had no direct interaction with the outside world. It required special permission from the Brazilian government and a health exam just to meet with this group of Sateré-Mawé. Permission to meet uncontacted tribes was even more difficult to receive, and film crews were blocked entirely at the time due to the unscrupulous practices of a production company who, a few months before, had been careless and inadvertently brought diseases with them which decimated a village. The Sateré-Mawé are a fascinating people with a long and rich history in the region. They are perhaps best known as the first people to cultivate guarana, an upper similar to caffeine and cocaine, and a staple of American "energy drinks," served most frequently throughout Brazil as a soda with the same name whose flavor is best described as "Dr. Pepper meets a spicy sarsaparilla." It is also the tribe that engages in the Tucandeira ceremony – the most extreme tribal initiation in the world.

The tribe, like most indigenous peoples, has a history of mistreatment from outsiders. They have grown to be insular and not trust even the few Westerners they allow into their village. They are friendly, but never really accept you. I wanted them to trust me enough to tell me their legends – legends that they don't normally share with outsiders. They have an incredibly detailed oral tradition from which we can learn an immense amount about many of the animals I was interested in. We were there for only two weeks, and if I wanted them to talk to me, I needed them to trust me, and quickly. I racked my brain to think of what I could do to show them I respected their culture, and to earn their respect; that I could make them comfortable sharing their stories. I kept coming back to the Tucandeira. If I wanted to hear their story, I had to become part of their story. I had to show them the respect they deserved.

Reasons why I should not do this ran through my head as I lay awake in my hammock on the deck of the boat under a neon green mosquito net that trailed on the floor. Maybe I *had* eaten fish that day. I really couldn't remember. The boat captain never did say why he asked me that. Would it make the ceremony dangerous – well, more dangerous? Would the protein in my system somehow affect my body's reaction to the venom?

Back in the UK, I had told Anna I probably wouldn't do it. But she knew how dynamic these shoots were. The best we had going into the field was a loose framework of what we were going to film, an outline of the journey – and we had one with and one without the bullet ants. This wasn't scripted television by any means, and we would film based on what did or did not happen the next day. I had promised Anna to use my best judgment. I never actually said I *wasn't* going to do it, so this was not a reason to call it quits.

I hadn't changed my clothes in six days, not even my boxer-briefs or socks. While this was also not really a reason to not go through with it, the fact that my luggage was currently un-locatable – "They think it's on a boat near Codajas" was all that Sol, our incredible Brazilian/Bristolian associate producer for this shoot, could get from the airport staff on our satellite phone – was definitely on my mind that night. I didn't care about being stinky – I had some prescription painkillers in that luggage that I was counting on for the day after the ceremony.

Another mental argument was that my entire torso was covered in a disgusting and increasingly itchy rash that no one seemed to agree on the origin of. My travel-seasoned friend, our soundman James, thought it was a reaction to the malaria medication and suggested I stop taking them. "The strain of malaria in this region isn't too bad, mate, you'll be fine." Did I mention James was fairly hardcore? The most positive person I've ever met, James was the sound recordist for every episode of *Beast Hunter*. He is five years younger than me, exceptionally handsome, blond haired, blue eyed, scruffy bearded, incredibly bright, has been everywhere and seen everything, and is nearly always in a fantastic mood. Basically, everyone at Icon is amazing, and some of the greatest, most talented people I've ever come across. Even among this group of superhumans, James is a standout. Not only is he talented in literally all aspects of production (he directs, produces, edits, writes, is a cameraman, sound recordist, drone operator, first responder, and general tech for all equipment), he's an amazing guy and a great friend. He's hysterically funny – *very* inappropriate, but extremely respectful to every person he comes into contact with. He always asks for people's names and actually listens and pays attention to whomever he is speaking with. His partner, Jen, is just as kind, talented, and wonderful, and they have two amazing girls who will probably never know how lucky they are to have these two as their parents. As great as he is, I was not planning on taking his medical advice.

Sol thought it looked "like… a bite from a… something. Or maybe a reaction from that bite?" We had been filming at a village earlier that night on our way to Sateré-Mawé and were swarmed by night wasps – evil insects that leave horrible itchy welts after painful stings. But I was itchy and rashy all over my torso – not near the night-wasp stings on my forearms. It went from annoying to unbearable in the span of an hour.

Ben, our snappily dressed leader and producer, thought it was from the tarantula the night before. "Those little hairs of theirs are buggers. They puff 'em all over you if you mess with them, and you, sir, messed with 'em." He was right – I had caught a tarantula and played with it for a while, before turning it over to our contacts at the tribe and watching, in shocked fascination, as they skewered it and roasted it over a fire, urticating hairs sizzling and filling the air with an acrid smoke. It didn't taste half-bad though. Like crab, really, if you ignored the burnt hair smell and crunchy exoskeleton.

In order to participate in the ceremony, our insurance company required that we hire a local emergency medic who would have a medivac helicopter available should I need it.

Up until this point, he had enjoyed smoking and strutting around shirtless far too much to encourage my faith in him as a physician, but he cleared up the mystery with two words after I ripped my shirt off in frustration and reveled the extent of the rash – "chicken mites."

"You were around chickens, yes?"

Yes, for the last three days I had been around chickens.

"You sat in the dirt near the chickens, maybe held one to your head?"

No, I had not held a chicken to my head, why would I hold a chicken to my head? But yes, I sat in the dirt near them.

"Chicken mites. They stay with you two weeks, living in your skin, then fall out and die. Don't scratch them or they die in you and rot and you get an infection."

No scratching the thousands of little bugs living in my skin. Done. After hearing the diagnosis, one of our guides just said "Oh no, that's not fun," and produced some medicinal smelling ointment which took the edge off the itching. He was a member of a different local tribe and had some great traditional remedies.

Again, I had to admit, while very uncomfortable, the chicken mites were not a reason to skip the ceremony. Plus, I had gained a little weight before this shoot and knew the ceremony would probably require me to be at least shirtless, maybe even more naked, and with the chicken mites I could chalk up my pasty-flab to swelling caused by the parasites infecting me if it got mentioned on blogs, so, really, the chicken mites were kind of a plus, in a very narcissistic way.

Were the mites a sign, though? Was this an indication that the insects of Brazil didn't want me there? Should I walk away, go to the "fallback" script?

Sol thought so. "Pat, what is *wrong* with you? Don't do this. Seriously." Sol was kind of the mom of the group. She treated us like her boys, even if she was younger than most of us (James was the baby of the team, still in his early twenties). Sol, like everyone else at Icon, is incredible. Aside from being a world-class AP and fixer, she's brilliant and beautiful, with olive skin, huge dark eyes, long dark wavy/curly hair, and an incredible accent showing signs of her upbringing between Sao Paulo and Bristol. She had all of the proportions of a Brazilian model minus the height – but, even at only 5'4", she was a force to be reckoned with. She had the fiery temper and fierce loyalty Brazilian women are famous for with the partying attitude of a Bristolian uni student. There was something incredibly comforting about Sol's presence in the group – you felt there was someone there who was always protecting you and would make everything okay.

Ben seemed to be the only one besides me in the YOLO school of bullet ants. His thought, like mine, was that this was the opportunity of a lifetime, and I'd regret *not* doing it forever, whereas I'd only regret actually doing it for a few days – a few months, at the longest. As long as I survived. He said he was even considering joining me, just with one sting, to say he'd done it.

Your grandmother would describe Ben as "devilishly handsome," and, with a smile and blush, tell you to "watch out with that one." He has a perpetual look of mischief about him, like any minute he might shout "got you!", and something you'd taken for granted, like his name and age, would be revealed as incorrect. I wouldn't be at all surprised if, the next time I see Ben, I find out he's actually a middle-aged Brazilian man named Jao – he would explain this in a thick Portuguese accent revealed to be his real voice. Ben (Jao) would remain a very close friend even after this revelation because Ben is incredible. There's also a slight chance that he is the elusive Bristolian street artist Banksy.

He's ageless. Again, if it was revealed that he was either in his twenties or his forties I wouldn't be surprised. He has a runner's build and is an avid biker. His complexion is dark and swarthy but his eyes are light, almost a yellowish tan ringed by a vibrant and captivating dark green. He's usually a bit scruffy and definitely looks the part of "explorer." You can tell before he opens his mouth that he has the best stories of anyone in the room, and he absolutely does.

Ben has been everywhere and done everything. I won't attempt to tell any of his stories here, but will say he's wrangled wild Komodo dragons and spent time in an Afghan prison after illegally breaking into an abandoned Soviet-era biological weapons facility for a documentary. Unlike many people in the exploring industry, Ben's stories aren't brimming at the surface and usually require a few drinks and some quiet pauses before they come to light, which makes them more exciting. Ben is not a guy who can't wait to share and attempt to one-up someone during a raucous conversation, although he easily could. He's a musician and a wonderful father to two incredible boys, one who looks like a mini-Ben, and a younger one who is perhaps double his brother's size, blond, and displays the Irish complexion of Ben's incredible partner.

Ben frequently wears Ben Sherman and other hipster-chic brands in the jungles and forests and avoids having his photo taken at all costs. He is extremely "cool," and I mean that in the best possible way. I think everyone who knows him admires him and tries to emulate him in a way usually reserved for older brothers or your older sister's boyfriend. At one point we were being eaten alive by insects in Brazil, covered in mosquitos and bees. The sweat bees were particularly nasty because they would give tiny annoying stings causing you to swat them, and the resulting gory mess would stink like old fish and attract even more bees. I offered Ben my spare insect-proof head covering – basically a mesh bag that went over your head. Ben seemed delighted and grateful, then went to put it on, feigning a struggle to get it over his head. Grunting in exaggerated exhaustion and miming the inability to pull it over himself, he handed it back and said, "Sorry, mate, I physically can't wear anything that lame. My body rejected it."

Ben works extremely hard at appearing to not work at all. He would stay awake hours after all of us planning out the next day's shots then downplay the importance of each, saying: "I think it might look good if we X, but whatever you feel would be best, TV's Pat Spain." Or "Right, so, the way I see it, if we do X, we won't need to work the rest of the day, yeah?" In reality, Ben never took time off. He was always working, and all of us wanted to please him. Every idea he had for a shot was brilliant, and the only hard part was keeping him reined in, which was Laura's job. The rest of us just enjoyed the ride that was being in Ben's company.

Ben normally seems nonplussed about everything, taking it all in his stride. He doesn't sugarcoat either, which I always appreciate. When I would flub a scene, Ben would say, "Right, that was shit. Do it again, but better, yeah?" with a huge smile. He generally has a big smirk and appears to be taking everything in, but staying unaffected by it. To say he is unimpressed would be incorrect – he seems equally impressed by everything. Like, we might all be gathered, admiring a gorgeous sunset over the Amazon river, when Ben would walk over and join us after working on tweaks to a script and say, earnestly if distractedly, "Wow, pretty, yeah?" with a jutting bottom lip and a slightly impressed head nod. Then, without pausing, "All right, so what I'm thinking for tomorrow is..." You rarely got more praise than that. This was a side effect of having been everywhere and done everything. He had truly seen it all before, and although he did appreciate it, he was not often moved in the way most humans are.

James and Brendan (camera) were a little less concerned than Sol, but agreed with her on the whole. "Pat, this is *mental*, mate. Jen [James' beautiful, funny, and easygoing BBC-employed partner] worked on the Backshall episode. She said it traumatized the *crew*, much less what it did to poor Steve."

"Yeah, Pat. Steve's a big guy, and don't take this the wrong way, but you don't exactly look like a warrior," chimed in Brendan, unnecessarily.

Brendan is a well-known high-fashion photographer and the cameraman for nearly every episode of *Austin Stevens: Snake Master* and quite a few episodes of *River Monsters*. In a given week he can go from shooting nude supermodels having a glitter fight in London (true story) to filming an extremely dirty young man catching snakes in a distant jungle, both in 3D! He's South African, was arrested for protesting against Apartheid, and has lived everywhere including Pakistan (which he says is gorgeous) and Afghanistan (which he has less nice things to say about). Brendan is talented and worldly enough that he would be able to get away with being extremely pretentious, but he isn't. He's quiet, a little goofy and thoughtful, and someone who is just interesting to talk to about anything. His favorite topics are cinematography, which he can really geek out on, and his kids.

The Tucandeira ceremony is an ancient rite of passage for young men or women (almost always men, however) who want to earn the right to be a hunter, the highest social-class in their society. It used to be warriors, but luckily the tribe hasn't needed warriors in many years, so it's now hunters who have the best marriages, the most respect, the best places to live, etc. Those individuals intent on earning this place in society must endure the ritual twenty times over the course of a few years without making a sound. The reasoning goes that if you can do the bullet ants twenty times, you can do anything. If you were out hunting and a wild boar gored you, you might think, "Oh my *GOD*! This is the *WORST*! I'm just going to lie down and die." But, if you've done the bullet ants twenty times, your reaction would be more, "'Tis only a flesh wound," and you'd walk back to the village for treatment.

Few make it through the ritual to the end. Many never attempt it, others give up after a few goes, and some, like our boat captain, after one. I would be doing it once and, I hoped, showing them that I respected their traditions, thus gaining their respect, seeing the jungle from their perspective, and earning the privilege of hearing the stories they rarely shared with non-tribe members.

My final, and most convincing, reason not to do it was, quite simply, how terrible it was going to be, and after that horror it might not even work as intended. I might go through with it and they still wouldn't trust me, would still see me as another outsider who'd come to exploit them, rather than to prove my respect for their culture. I can't stress enough that this was not a stunt. I genuinely wanted to show respect and reverence for their way of life by participating in it fully. It was going to be *really* terrible, though. I could die – we had heard stories about people actually dying from bullet ant stings – and if I didn't, it might have permanent mental effects. PTSD and death were both on my mind as I lay there feeling the rocking of the boat and hearing the muffled snores of my friends. I'd later find out that Ben was more nervous than I was that night, believing that his encouragement would cause my death, and didn't sleep a wink.

I woke up the morning of the ceremony not feeling very well rested. I'm not sure if it was the hammock, the mites, my nerves, or a combination of the three, but I barely got four hours of sleep, and it was fitful. I had some tapioca pancakes with condensed milk and fresh fruit that tasted like it had been picked minutes before I ate it, which it probably had. I also drank a large quantity of guarana soda, which I am convinced has not only uppers but also anti-depressants in it. It was too hot to drink coffee, so a few glasses of guarana before 8 am was normal for a morning in Brazil.

I was feeling a good buzz by the time Ben said we had better be off. The entire village had been told that an outsider would be taking part in the Tucandeira ritual and they were gathered on the shore when we got off the boat. I know there are tribes somewhere who still wear grass skirts, penis gourds, or animal feathers as everyday wear, but I've never seen them. The indigenous peoples I've met wear the preferred clothes of most people around the world – Adidas track pants, once brightly colored and now faded T-shirts, flip-flops, and baseball caps. Yes, some of the T-shirts are the famous "Dewey Defeats Truman"-esque misreported sporting events (Patriots super bowl champs, 2008, etc.), but most are simply solid or stripes that have faded to a well-worn gray. All of these tribes put on "traditional" clothes for three reasons: ceremony (sort of like us wearing a tux), tourists, or film crews. The cameras come out and people vanish, only to reappear grinning in an accommodating "I know this what you want" kind of way, shirtless, and with their genitals loosely covered by some vegetation. I have often found the time I spend off-camera with the tribes much more interesting than what we filmed, including the dress.

I once spoke to a man in the Congo about chickens who was wearing a "Jon Cena" T-shirt ("Because he looks like a tough man, and I am a tough man. People see him and know this is the type of man I am," he told me), Guess jeans, and a flat cap, who also happened to have facial tattoos and teeth filed to points. I learned a lot about the birds from him. Many in that tribe had face tats and filed teeth but wore Western clothes.

The Sateré-Mawé mixed traditional and Western styles in an amazing and slightly disconcerting way. The clothes were all Western, no pandering to the cameras, which I liked, but there was also a lot of body paint – every-day and ceremonial – feathers, and piercings.

One particular young man had very elaborate midnight-blue decorations on his arms and legs depicting a night scene – moon, stars, swirling night-winds, waves, swaying trees, birds, and, of course, ants. I asked about it, complimenting the incredible designs, and was told that his girlfriend had done it in celebration of his twentieth and, hopefully, final Tucandeira. He was very good looking with strong, defined facial features, thick hair with some sort of product to spike it, tanned skin, and very dark and piercing eyes. He was also jacked – I mean, he had Taylor Lautner-esque abs – and moved like an MMA fighter with complete control over his entire body, with lightning-fast reflexes. His girlfriend was, unsurprisingly, incredibly beautiful in ripped jeans and a black tank top but shyer than him, just peeking to get a glimpse of us, then giggling and running away as she waved her dye-stained hands in a flustered motion at our cameras. I'm guessing they were both around 18 and were clearly the equivalent of the captain of the football team and head cheerleader in this tribe. This analogy was strengthened when I was told he was the one to watch during the ceremony that day. Apparently, his mastery of pain was unparalleled, and he was likely the next "chief," or leader. I never fully understood how this position was bestowed, or when, but it was assumed by all that he was next, and this assumption seemed to be based on his performances during previous rituals.

The two other painted men who would be joining us in the ritual did not look nearly as collected as him. They fidgeted, tried to joke with each other, failed, then fidgeted some more. I was told that day would be number four and twelve for these guys, who were both around 16. None of the three of them seemed to care very much about us being there – they were in their own heads, mentally preparing. They wore board shorts, flip-flops, and nothing else.

We made our introductions to the village elder or chief. He was old, hunched, and wore baggy canvas cargo pants and a faded polo shirt. He was wrinkled and smiled a lot – it was a warm smile, but you could tell he was a powerful, strong, and proud man. He said I was welcome to join in the ceremony. He was proud to share it with someone from the outside world. He said it was an important part of their culture and thanked me for showing them respect by doing it. He told me that, if I went through with it, I would be one of them, and the forest would be open to me – when I could function again, he didn't need to add.

"If I went through with it." When he said that I realized that no one expected me to actually do this. Not our crew, not anyone at Icon, not Anna, not even the Sateré-Mawé themselves. No one really thought I'd do it.

At that point, a few of the guys in the tribe who looked to be in their early twenties started giving me shit. They said, through our translator, that there was no way I would go through with it. They said the pain from one sting would be enough to make me curl up and cry like a baby. Honestly, I was concerned they were right. I really don't like pain, and this was going to be awful. The chief told them to shut up and play nice, and for the most part they did. They actually started psyching me up then, telling me they had all done it and it would be really cool if I did too because I'd be one of them. Turns out they were the cool-kid clique – the hunters, the ones who had completed the ritual – they had earned the right to give anyone they wanted shit, unless the chief shut it down. They started teasing me, playfully, but were actually being really nice, like the cool older brother every guy wishes they had. The guy who would sucker punch you, but in a "You're one of the guys" kind of way.

They all did this, except for one smarmy prick. This one kid just seemed to have a chip on his shoulder. Let's call him "Bret" for ease of reference. He went out of his way to intimidate me or make me look bad – tripping me, "accidentally" spilling on me, constantly talking about how painful the bullet ants are – you know, classic Bret. The other guys basically told me to ignore him, and I tried, though unsuccessfully.

Far too soon it was time to collect the ants. I'm not sure if people are completely aware of this, but there are a *lot* of insects in the Amazon basin. I know bugs, and I love bugs. My niece and nephew call me "Uncle Bug" because I'm always catching bugs and talking about them, but I have never experienced bugs like I did in the Brazilian Amazon. Most of the time we were in the forest we were covered in sweat bees – thousands of them. It got to be the running joke: "cue the bees" one of us would say, or, "I see James remembered to bring the bees. Thanks for that." By the end of the shoot it had turned into, "Can someone tell the bees they're done for the day?", or simply, "God I really hate these fucking bees!" The sweat bee stings were more of an annoyance than they were painful. What really sucked was that, if you squashed one, the resulting goo smelled like rotten fish and drew more bees to the scent. Also, they seemed to love the corners of the eyes. It was like a lacrimal caruncle was Mecca and, at some point before their death, they had to make their way to it, at all costs.

In addition to the bees (I really can't emphasize enough how many there were), there were massive stick bugs, huge leaf insects, giant tarantulas (which I know are not insects, but are "bugs"), tailless jungle scorpions, and lots of other creepy crawlies that I managed to find and catch, or, like the chicken mites and night bees, that managed to find and catch me.

This walk in the woods was no different. There were bees, spiders, mosquitoes, and more. The hunters we were with seemed unperturbed. They were focused on the task at hand and periodically blew a note from a carved-bamboo wind instrument they each carried. They said it was for "protection" – spiritual and physical – while gathering the ants. I was itchy, anxious, and getting very nervous – protection sounded nice but, honestly, I just wanted to get on with it and did not appreciate the random, jarringly loud notes that periodically emanated from the men, breaking what little concentration I had. It was about 102ºC with 90% humidity, and hunter-douche Bret wasn't making the walk any more enjoyable. He kept flicking little pieces of wood at me to make me think bugs were landing on me, then laughing and shouting, "Look how much he flinches! He's never going to do the Tucandeira! He'll wimp out, you just watch. He'll get his little test-sting and run back to his mommy." He said this while looking at Sol, who shot him her Brazilian death stare. Sol is super friendly, funny, smart, etc., but when he's angry it's like a switch has been flipped. I would never want to be on the receiving end of the stare that guy earned. It shut him up for a little while, but once we got to the ants, he started up again. Finally, his friends got him to shut up as I think even they were getting sick of his shit, or they wanted to impress Sol, maybe both. (I found out later that he had technically completed the full ritual the requisite twenty times, but had been forced to repeat ten of them. Although no one would say it, this probably meant he had yelled out during the ceremony, and maybe this left him feeling like he always had something to prove to the other hunters, most of whom completed each ritual without incident.)

We reached a tree that had been scouted a couple of days before and identified as a bullet-ant site. The ants make their nest underground at the base of a tree but travel to and from the canopy multiple times a day in search of food. Their incredibly potent sting is used as a deterrent and in defense of their home tree rather than as a means to subdue or kill potential prey. They generally eat nectar, sap, and other insects. Once we arrived, a few of the hunters started hitting the tree with sticks. This caused an "all-hands-on-deck" response from the ants, who poured to the site of the "attack" from above and below in droves. We each had long bamboo sticks that we put in front of the ants, who defended their home tree in a fury, biting and stinging the stick. They climbed onto it in their attempt to kill it, and we'd then put the stick, with the ants still biting and stinging it, in a large bamboo tube, shake and twist the stick to get them to let go, and trap them in the tube.

The guy holding the tube had the most dangerous job. I saw a few ants fall from their stick and land on him, but he managed to shake them all off without getting stung. He not only had to hold the bamboo containing the ants, but was responsible for occasionally tapping it on the ground to keep any of the collected insects from crawling out.

One older guy took one of the ants and cut its stinger off with a knife, then held it to my face for me to examine as it bit into his calloused hand and drew blood. It was the first time I saw one up close. It was huge, a monster insect, really more of a wingless wasp than an ant. The Brazilian ants are the largest phenotype of bullet ants, much bigger than the ones I'd seen in Costa Rica. It was a gun-metal black with golden legs and antennae. Its body was divided into four long segments. Its head was equipped with massive, powerful jaws apparently capable of drawing blood. The segment after the head (the mesosoma — or thorax) was oddly shaped; it looked like a saddle with two horns protruding from it. The beast seemed ready for some tiny demon to use as its steed, riding on this natural saddle. After the saddle came a short, thin, thorny-looking bit, then the oversized abdomen (or gaster), which looked like two bulbous pustules stuck together and tapering to a horribly long point, the stinger – which had been removed, but was clearly visible on the other scurrying ants – like a black needle sticking out of these cenobite creatures. This ant, which was still ripping into this guy's hand, appeared to be growling or hissing at him. The first time I heard it I didn't think it could possibly be the ant, but it was. These ants hiss and growl at you. How terrifying and evil is that? We collected well over a hundred ants and, after the first five dozen, each time we put one in I thought, "Okay, that must be enough" – and then we got more.

When the eldest hunter determined we'd collected enough, the tube-holder capped it and shook the audibly irritated ants. The tube amplified the grunts and growls of the pissed-off beasts inside, and the resulting cacophony sounded like a mix of an angry hornet's nest and a rabid raccoon.

As we walked back, I noticed for the first time how much taller I was than any of the other hunters, and, more significantly, how much larger my hands were. Most initiates were still in their teens and their hands were significantly smaller than mine. This would probably give them the advantage of only contacting about half of the ants! I, like Backshall before me, would theoretically get double the stings, as well as stings from "fresh" ants – the thought amongst those who have done the ritual is that the first person gets the worst of it because the ants are "fresh." Some researchers say it doesn't really matter, but the thought was in my head. As the "guest," I would be going either first or last. I was really hoping for last. Generally, they went "new guys first," but no one expected much from me and the star of the day was expected to be the next-in-line chief, so they determined they'd let me go last and the future chief could pick his spot. He chose second in line.

The young hunters told me about a certain way to hold your hands in order to minimize contact with the ants. I held my hands up, palm to palm against one of theirs, and said that I didn't think I would have that option. They all started laughing. I smiled, but saw nothing funny about it – shit was getting real. They said to try and press the backs of my hands into the gloves so as not to get stung on my palms. I thought I could at least try this. If you curl your hand, forming a canoe, and place your thumbs over your palms it was supposed to protect the most sensitive part of your hands – your inner palms – they said. I thanked them and said I'd try it out. (Spoiler alert – it didn't work.)

As we re-entered the village, ants in hand, so to speak, they led me to the hut where the ceremony was set to take place. It was completely open with no walls, just a thatched roof with poles holding it up. In the center was a long, wrist-thick stick propped up to about belly-button height on me (chest height on the other initiates) by crossed sticks on either side. It looked like a thin balancing beam. As I stared, unable to focus, the chief brought out the ceremonial gloves and my heart started racing. They were beautiful and ancient looking; a rusted, faded, blood-red plant material was woven between straw colored raffia leaves in an intricate tribal pattern that evoked a primal sense of respect and reverence in everyone who looked at them. There were tall orangey-red, white, gray, and blue, ancient-looking feathers coming from the top. The gloves were an elongated hexagonal shape, like how a little-kid would draw a tall house with a steep roof. There were also gloves inside of these gloves.

The inner gloves lacked the intricate color pattern and stylization, but were similarly shaped, and newer looking. They were the greenish-tan of semi-fresh raffia leaves and their weave was a bit looser. These were the gloves that would hold the ants. It made sense – the inner gloves contain the ants, the outer gloves are larger and allow the chief to place them on and take them off each initiate without the risk of being stung. Unless an ant escaped – the hunters delighted in telling me stories of ants getting loose and crawling onto initiates' faces, stinging the entire way. The same rules applied if that happened – dance with the chief and the other initiates, don't cry out, don't flinch and, don't swat at them.

An elder member of the tribe brought out a large metal pot with about three inches of clear liquid and some leaves in it. I was told this was the solution that would render the ants unconscious. They'd be out for about two hours, which would give us time to prep our equipment, eat (no meat for me, I was told again), get me painted, have my required "tester" sting, and mentally ready myself for the ceremony – if I still decided I wanted to go through with it after the test sting, that is.

Different groups of Sateré-Mawé carry out the body-painting

portion of the ceremony in unique ways based on the resources of the area. Some groups apply a thin layer of ash in patterns all over the initiate's body, hands, and arms. The ash is supposed to provide some protection as it's said to confuse the ants. I'm told this is a myth, and the ants are just as potent, ash or no ash. The group I was with was a "no ash" group. They used the juice of a particular fruit to create beautiful midnight-blue patterns on the initiate's bodies to symbolize different aspects of their jungle home. The juice went on clear, but within four or five hours it oxidized and revealed the patterns that the initiates' loved ones had drawn. This was generally done the day before, but not in my case as no one was convinced I'd actually be doing it. They had decided to wait until the point of no return to paint me. No one other than the initiates were allowed to wear the body paint as it signified to all who saw it – in the tribe and elsewhere – that the person donning it was to be respected, and had committed to the Tucandeira. I suddenly understood how important the blue hands of the future-chief's girlfriend were. She had been allowed to paint him for this important last ritual and had chosen a night scene – very telling in the young lovers' lives. I had a feeling this night wouldn't be *all* bad for him.

Many young kids in the tribe gathered around to watch as the hunters emptied the collected ants into the pot. There was a lot of excited giggling and yelling as a few ants missed the pot and started charging at people. Ben reminded me that we needed one alive and conscious and produced an empty plastic guarana bottle. He asked me to collect one and put it in. I did and the bottle's hour-glass shape distorted the massive insect into even stranger proportions. I held it up, studying it. It was *pissed*, trying to bite and sting the bottle. I saw tiny droplets of venom where it pressed its impressive, needle-like stinger into the plastic. I couldn't believe I was looking at an ant. The bottle seemed to vibrate with its aggression and anger.

As the ants in the pot started to pass out, an elder tribe

member started weaving them into the gloves with the help of a couple of young boys with hunter ambitions, which is when Bret started in again, saying: "The pain is enormous. Just you wait. You can't do it and I will make sure of it. I'm going to make sure it really hurts you, and you have to dance longer and have the ants pressed into your palms, because you are a fake and can't handle this." The other hunters looked away, a little embarrassed for him. Sol got very angry and yelled at him, "Fuck off and leave us alone. You aren't chief and can't do anything to control how the ceremony goes."

He walked away grinning. Sol then asked the chief, who was standing just out of earshot of Bret's taunts, if there was any way they could go light on me. She asked if I could have less ants, or wear the gloves for a shorter amount of time, or anything that might help. The chief smiled kindly and explained this was an "all or nothing thing." He said he hoped I would respect them and do the ceremony, but also hoped that I would understand that this was an ancient ritual and could not be altered for our purposes. He said he would not be offended if I didn't do it, but if I did, it had to be the whole thing. Sol apologized and explained that of course they understood, and she was asking on her own initiative, that I hadn't asked her to speak on my behalf. The chief again smiled and said he knew that, she was just "concerned for her friend's safety," and had good reason to be. This was not something to enter lightly, and advised me to really think about it before I was painted.

I ate a few bites of a vegetarian meal in near silence. The crew wouldn't look me in the eyes. I tried to joke a little but wasn't really feeling it. Sol was nearly in tears. My heart was racing and my stomach was doing flips. I started to worry I was going to have to back out. I pulled Ben aside and told him how scared I was. He admitted he was just as scared, and said, "Maybe this was a stupid idea." He told me not to worry if I didn't want to do it. I said that I at least wanted to do the tester ant, and Ben said, "Yeah, okay, brilliant," but his previous enthusiasm was gone.

Ben got the doctor just as a couple of hunters came by and said the ceremony would be starting in about 30 minutes as the ants were starting to twitch. They explained that the two-hour estimate was very rough and "these ants were anxious." Great news, anxious bullet ants – just what I needed to hear right then. The doctor came at a brisk jog, shirtless again and heavily perfumed. What was with this dude? He said that 30 minutes would be okay as anaphylaxis generally set in "real quick" if it was going to happen.

All of this seemed like it was happening too fast. I kept thinking, "Am I just nervous, or is this the 'bad feeling' Anna asked me to listen to?" I was so confused and nervous I really couldn't tell.

Brandon and James indicated that they were ready to film, then Ben handed me the guarana bottle with the ant in it, averting his eyes. His hand was shaking and he looked pale. "Good luck, mate. You don't have to do this," was all he could say. I nodded and unscrewed the cap. I looked at James – sound was up – and Brendan – camera was rolling. I planned to get stung on my left arm, but at the last moment thought, "Why minimize the pain? If this is a tester, I may as well see what it's really going to feel like." So I shook the ant out of the bottle onto my left hand.

The rest of this chapter is based on my notes, written three days after the ceremony when I was able to hold a pen again. They represent my best recollections, but there are stretches of blank space that I had to ask the crew to fill in. Reality started to blur right after the test-sting. I can't distinguish fully between what was really happening and what was only in my mind.

A few little kids had gathered around to watch, grinning and laughing, and once the ant started crawling around on me, they gave a collective "Ouuuuuuuuuuuhhhh." The rest of the tribe were in the ceremonial hut while the crew and I were in what looked like an open-air classroom, complete with desks and a blackboard, but again no walls. The ant was really amped up after spending some time in the bottle and started biting me right away. I instinctively yelled "Ow!" after one good bite and the little kids broke into hysterics. I had already forgotten the "no yelling" rule – good thing this wasn't the real ceremony. I kind of smiled along with them, despite the situation. I realized that I could actually feel the weight of the ant on my hand, it was that big. Also, each leg seemed to have a barb on it that dug into my skin and scratched it, a couple of footsteps even drawing little drops of blood. I tried prodding it with the stick to get it to sting, but very few insects will sting what they are standing on. Instead, it started grunting. Now that it was on me, I could really hear it. It wasn't a clicking of its exoskeleton like some insects make, it sounded like an actual hissing or grunting vocalization. It is stridulation – sound produced by rubbing various body parts together – but my God it sounded like it was growling at me. It crawled onto my palm and I instinctively moved my hand to shake it off. Then it happened.

"Fuck! Shit! Shit! Oh my God! Fuck!" There was more laughter from the kids – I had again broken the "no yelling rule." It was my left hand – between my thumb and wrist, a good meaty part of my hand, probably the least painful spot you can get stung on your hands – and it was terrible.

I've been stung or bitten by just about anything you can think of: pythons, a rattlesnake, siafu ants, a rabid raccoon, a small bear, every species of hornet, bee and wasp in the northeast US – even multiple species at once, with multiple individuals of each species. I've had jellyfish stings in my eyes, up my nose, in my mouth, down my bathing suit. Basically, what I'm saying is, I am no stranger to the pain an animal can cause, but nothing, I mean nothing, can come close to the pain from a single bullet-ant sting. The best way to describe the initial feeling is like a thick-gauged needle injecting sulfuric acid into your hand, which then gets worse.

It was an intense fiery pain. I have spilled very strong hydrochloric and sulfuric acid on my hands on a few occasions during my time in bio and chem labs, but this was like having it injected subcutaneously. The sting itself, the actual injection, was horrible, worse than a huge needle, and then there was the venom, which I could *feel* enter my system, flowing in hot, rhythmic pulses. I could see the ant's bulbous abdomen pulsing and pumping, like a diseased heart. I started sweating and the world went quiet. It was horrifying. I lost the ability to move my thumb almost instantly. The pain started to spread but it was a weird pain, not something you would want to put pressure on, or leave exposed. It was just terrible. It was under the skin, insidious, something you just know is doing untold horrors to your nerves but there's no way you can stop it.

Within minutes I was pacing, laughing maniacally because I didn't know what else to do. It was like I'd slammed my hand in a door, over and over and over again, and it never let up. There was no position I could put my hand in to make it better, and it just kept getting worse. Every 30 seconds or so I would realize how much worse it was than a little while before. I started hallucinating and gasping for breath, as the pain had actually taken my breath away. I was breathing fast and the doctor started to check me. He smiled and said it wasn't an allergic reaction. I was just experiencing a shock-like reaction from the trauma. It wasn't a sharp pain (after the initial sting), but I couldn't call it dull either, just constant and unrelenting, like no other pain I've ever experienced.

The shirtless, smoking doctor was monitoring me and saying I was okay. The ritual was about to start, the initiates were lined up and ready to begin without me. I was going to have to decide if I was going to participate, now. The doctor wasn't going to get any more time to monitor me, but he thought I'd be okay based on the last 20 minutes.

"God," I thought. "Has it already been twenty minutes?" Time seemed to be moving differently. I tried to describe the pain to camera, but found it hard to express my thoughts in words. Instead, I ended up staring, believing I could convey messages telepathically.

We started walking towards the ceremonial tent and I pulled Ben aside and said I didn't think I could do it. This was only one sting and I was in agony, more pain than I'd ever experienced. I was already having mild hallucinations, feeling like my body was trying to remove my mind from reality.

Ben understood, and actually said, "Fuck, thank you for saying that. I think this is for the best," then said we would still film the ritual and asked if I wanted to watch. I nodded, closing my eyes and trying to will the pain away.

Ben asked if there was anything he could do to help me, and I shook my head. There wasn't, and I couldn't speak anyway. I was *in* the pain, experiencing it fully. I was pouring sweat. I tried speaking without using words, thinking I was talking to Ben, telling him this had been my decision and I didn't blame him, but nothing was coming out of my mouth. He gave me a little one-armed hug and just said, "Hang in there, mate, it'll be okay."

Then I saw the initiates, lined up, facing forward, ready for much worse than one sting. They had primeval looking percussion instruments tied to their legs, like rattles. They also had additional red-clay paint in intricate patterns overlaid on the midnight blue I'd seen before. I saw the looks of determination on their faces – they knew what they were about to go through, and they were still there, ready to face it.

Then I saw Bret, he was grinning an oily looking smirk. He started elbowing the other hunters and pointing at me saying, "Told you! I knew it. I knew he was a fake. I knew he wouldn't do it." I saw the chief look at me and give a kind, knowing, smile. He nodded and shrugged, seeming to say, "It's okay, I understand." Then I looked back at Bret, looking smug and making faces at Sol, who ignored him. He came over to me and said something, knowing I couldn't understand. Ben shook his head in disgust and told me to ignore him, then asked what I was thinking.

"Fuck it. I'm going to do it," I said, and started unbuttoning my shirt.

"What? I thought you were going to sit it out?"

"I can see the looks on all of their faces. They're going to think I have no respect for them, that I'm a fucking tourist. They'll never trust me."

"Pat, don't worry about it. We'll have a good show without this."

"But it'll be *great* with it. I didn't come all this way, plan this for weeks, bring a doctor on the shoot, and everything else we did to prep to *not* do this. The stories we'll hear from them? The respect I'll get for our whole crew? I'm doing it. This is my decision, Ben. I'm doing it, and it'll be worth it."

Ben just stood there, stunned, clearly unsure what to say or do. It was the only time I've ever seen him unsure of anything. Finally, he leaned in close to me and just said, "*This* is the scene that everyone will remember," and told Brendan to film me. He then asked Sol to ask the tribe to prep me.

My shirt was off and James was trying to rig a lav-mic to me somehow. My hand was throbbing and I was still dripping sweat, but I had a massive surge of adrenaline and was finding it difficult to stay still. I was moving from leg to leg, breathing in shallow gasps, really expelling the air like I was trying to blow out the pain. My brow was furrowed and I was ready.

Bret looked disappointed for a second, then grinned as he was asked to be the one to prep me. He laughed as he grabbed my stung hand to check it out. He wanted me to flinch, and wasn't disappointed. His touch sent a wave of pain through my body, but I managed to not yell. He slapped my hand and said, "Feels good, yeah?" Ben and Sol asked if the red and blue paints could be applied like the other initiates – on my hands, legs, and torso, but not my face. They didn't want my face blue in some shots and not in others. A lot of the footage we shot would be assembled out of sequence for the episode – this is one of the main reasons that a host wears the same outfit every day. He smiled and agreed, asking them to step back, saying the next part was for the initiates only. He grabbed a container of what looked like dirty dishwater but contained the juice which would turn my skin navy blue after a few hours and, smirking, sunk his hands into it and rubbed it all over my face and head, making a "blah" sound. No designs were drawn, he just took all of the juice and rubbed it on all of the exposed skin he could get to, then threw the rest of it at me. It was everywhere – on my pants, in my boots, all over my body, face, and head. He skipped the red paint altogether. Part of me wanted to punch him, but most of me didn't really care and just wanted to focus on what was about to happen.

He walked away chuckling, and then motioned for Sol and Ben to rejoin me before the ceremony. Ben walked over, clearly pissed, and said, "What is his fucking issue?", as he used his own shirt to wipe my face. I was sweating so much that a lot of the juice wasn't staying on my skin long enough to dye it. I also had on the lotion from the chicken mites, sunscreen, and bug spray which made the dye take on patterns naturally. It would be another few hours until we saw the real damage, but it was looking like I would appear less like an initiate of the Tucandeira ceremony and more like a slightly pudgy Na'vi. Right then, I just looked very frightened, dirty, sweaty, and in a lot of pain.

The ritual was seconds away from starting, and all three young men seemed unphased that I would be joining after all. There was some hesitation as they apparently hoped I'd take the first spot, but the chief quickly dispelled this and placed me at the end of the line. The first initiate stepped up, put his forearms against the horizontal bar, leaned down in a supplicating motion with one leg bent in a genuflection, both arms raised to the initiation leader, an elder of the tribe, who was wearing a sleeveless Brazil soccer shirt. This man would sing the ancient song of the ritual and lead us, the initiates, in the dance.

I've contacted dozens of translation services to find the real words for the ceremony and come up short each time. One told me it's a very rare dialect of the Sateré-Mawé language, which is a rare language in and of itself. They said if they could get a translation it would have to be this dialect into Sateré, then Portuguese, then English – I was willing to spring for it, but in the end they couldn't even complete the first part. I can still hear it, plain as day – repeating over and over.

While I couldn't find the lyrics, I did find a song from Glory Opera – a Brazilian "progressive metal band focused on Amazonian folklore" – singing about the ritual in an English-language song called "Tucandeira – Ants of Fire," the lyrics of which are super metal and pretty spot on, but, unfortunately, cannot legally be reprinted here so please, do yourself a favor and mix a caipirinha, let your hair blow in the breeze, and head over to YouTube to be transported to Amazonia via prog-metal.

The leader placed the gloves on the hands of the first initiate, who stood up, stomped out a rhythm with his foot, shaking the rattle-like primordial instruments, linked arms with the elder and the other initiates, and started dancing. The leader sang a rhythmic and ancient-sounding song, a haunting melody that still rings in my head. I'm sure the lyrics are even more metal than Ants of Fire. I linked arms with the person closest to me and tried to follow the dance.

After five minutes the song stopped, and the initiate leaned his forearms on the horizontal stick. The gloves were removed and he stepped back in line. He looked like he was in agony.

His head was rolling from side to side, his eyes were going in and out of focus as he made pained expressions, but he didn't utter a sound.

The second initiate stepped up. He cracked his knuckles, flexed his arms and abs like a karate champion facing his opponent and trying to psych them out, looked straight ahead, and the leader placed the gloves on his hands. His expression didn't change and he didn't blink. He just stood up, linked arms, and started dancing. His expression was one of intense concentration, but nothing more. He was sweating and focused. When the song ended, he bowed with his forearms on the bar and the gloves were removed. He didn't scream, and didn't even breath heavy; he didn't seem to feel anything. He actually made fists with both hands, cracking his knuckles, and bowed. This was the last time he would wear the gloves. He was now a hunter. We were told later that day that, during this last Tucandeira, he handled the pain better than anyone in the tribe had ever seen. The crowd murmured their respects. This was a man who had earned his place in their society, the bravest, toughest, young man in a crowd of the most intense people I have ever met. It was the third person's turn and he handled it much like the first, with more wincing and some sounds like a wounded animal, low, and barely audible if you weren't standing right next to him. Not enough to disqualify him, I was later told.

I was up next. My left hand had reached a degree of pain I hadn't known was possible. It felt like it was being torn apart. It was melting, shredding from the inside. It was pain beyond pain, and I was about to get countless more stings from the same animal.

Ben leaned in close to me and whispered that I really didn't need to do this. I shook my head, unable to speak. I wanted to get on with it – my mind was made up. I was there, I was a nature show host, I was experiencing things that most people had never even heard of and certainly wouldn't ever have the opportunity to do themselves, and I was painted – I was an initiate, and it was my turn to face the horror.

I stepped up and placed my forearms on the bar, shaking, cringing, sweat pouring from me, heart pounding out of control. I took a few huge but shallow breaths "HUH HUH HUH HUH," then nodded to the chief and he placed the gloves with force onto my hands. The first sting I felt was the tip of my left middle finger. The stinger had found the spot under my nail, in the ultra-sensitive flesh of my fingertip, a spot on your body with one of the highest concentration of nerves and pain receptors.

The world went silent. My immediate and absolute first thought was what an incredibly terrible idea this was. I distinctly remember thinking, "This was a fucking terrible mistake. What have I done?" It was pain like I can't describe, pain beyond measure. I cried out, a pitiful, baleful whimper. I couldn't help it. I think a few people laughed. When I watch it on camera, it's more of an exhale, a "huff," and not a yell, so the ritual would count towards my twenty if I was going that route. I was fully conscious, but wished I would pass out.

Each sting was distinct. I could feel the huge stingers jabbing, sticking in, wiggling and pulsating to push the most venom into the deepest places that they could penetrate, pulling out and jabbing again nearby, repeating the horrible process over and over. I felt a sting in the webbing between my ring and middle finger which sent a new sensation of pain shooting through my body. I felt another on my left palm, right over the tester sting. The two pains merged but remained distinct, one searing like it was melting the musculature of my hand, the new one sharp and intense like a nail driving into already injured flesh. The combination made me feel faint. I started to feel stings on my knuckles, all of my fingers, front and back, everywhere on the backs of my hands, under my pinkies – each sting somehow unique, each equally horrifying. I could count each one. I realized that I was still kneeling at the bar, staring straight ahead, breathing so hard I was spitting on each exhale. I regretted my decision to do this, regretted it so much, and realized that I was in far over my head. As the chief grabbed my armpit to help me stand, I noticed that the singing hadn't started yet, my five minutes hadn't begun, even though I had been kneeling for nearly a minute, transfixed by the terror I'd brought upon myself.

I stood and almost fell over. The chief and the other initiates grabbed my arms and began dancing with me. The singing was horrible. I just wanted it to stop.

From my notes:

I want to stop stomping and dancing, I can't focus on the rhythm, I can't think about anything but the pain. I start to fall; I can't stand up but I can't stop dancing. Finally, after I have no idea how long, I just stop moving, the other initiates finish the dance, finish the song, with me standing, swaying in place, not dancing, not stomping, not blinking, just staring ahead of me unable to do anything but live in the pain; living only in my own head. I don't know how long it's been, seconds, hours, I have no idea. I can't move, I am screaming in my mind, begging Ben to make it stop, begging the tribe to remove the gloves, but I'm not actually saying anything. They wait for me to make the next move and I realize somewhere in my mind I have to put my arm against the pole for them to take the gloves off.

I finally did this. I was having a very hard time breathing. They took the gloves off by first pressing the ants into my hands again, squeezing the gloves, then twisting them so they would have a chance to sting fresh spots on their way off. It felt like tiny fishhooks plunging into then immediately tearing out of my flesh, the barbed stingers gripping my skin as they were roughly jerked away. I grunted at this new pain, an animalistic, primal, low growl I was completely unable to contain. I expected to see trails of blood as they took the gloves away. I thought my hands would be torn to shreds, and was shocked that they still looked like my hands, physically unchanged.

I cried out, and I honestly don't know if it was in my mind or reality at that point. It isn't in the footage, so it must have been in my head. It's a terrifying prospect to think that one uncontrolled outburst was enough to negate the entire experience. At the time I couldn't think straight, and wasn't concerned if it counted or not. All I knew was the pain – pure, unspeakable, unthinkable pain, consuming everything. I couldn't move my hands, which no longer felt like hands or any part of me, but like torture devices that had been cruelly stapled to me, a container filled with boiling water, broken glass, and jagged needles.

I just wanted it to stop, but somehow it kept getting worse – the water getting hotter and the broken glass breaking into smaller and sharper pieces. Every passing second made it worse. The initiates and the chief grabbed me and miraculously brought me into step with them. I had to keep dancing and stomping, but I couldn't feel or hear anything but the pain. The chief was singing and dancing in rhythm with us, and when the song changed we kept dancing, but to a different rhythm. I hated the dancing and wanted to stop and be alone. Alone with my pain. The singing sounded like it was coming through earplugs. It was distorted and muffled, far away. Nothing existed but the pain, and it was still getting worse. I had no other thoughts, nothing but pure, unadulterated pain.

The dancing stopped and I nearly passed out. The pain was getting worse than I could have imagined. The water turned into lava, the broken glass into razor blades, and the needles into grinding teeth. Oddly, it wasn't spreading, and was concentrated on my hands only. I counted 32 distinct points – I know I got a lot more stings than that, but there were 32 points of distinct and unbearable pain.

With the dancing over, I was left not knowing what to do with my body. I hated the dancing but it had kept me occupied and taken up at least a small portion of my brain, but once it ended every neuron was devoted to the pain. Reality started to blur further. There was no way this amount of pain was real; my body couldn't *actually* be going through this.

I remember bits and pieces of the next few hours, but the crew had to fill in a lot of gaps. I get mixed up when I try to remember it. What really happened? What was just in my head? And what do I only know because the crew told me? I can't distinguish – basically, my memory goes from dancing to the following glimpses of consciousness. Each memory fades in from black, then out to black. The following is what happened over the next four hours:

- The dancing stops.
- I beg Ben to remove the gloves.
- Sol is crying.
- Brendon tries to hug me and I shove him away.
- The ground is covered in bullet ants, kids are picking them up and eating them while they laugh. Chickens are eating them also. I try to get the kids to leave the ants alone because they are dangerous, but they just laugh at me.
- A kid's fingers are bleeding and he is eating the ants with bloody fingers.
- I scream at the top of my lungs.
- I'm running as fast as I can away from the pain and the ants.
- The ants are covering my body, crawling all over me, biting and stinging me in the face and arms, but I can't swat them off because I don't have any hands.
- I do have hands, but I can't use them. They are a

deadweight that radiates pain like they are on fire.

- I again beg Ben to take the gloves off me. My hands are sweating because the gloves are so hot.
- I'm running again but I can see myself running. I'm looking at myself from a different perspective like I have a camera mounted on my shoulder pointed at my face in profile.
- I jump over a massive opening in the ground, something like an old well.
- "Please take the gloves off, I don't want to do this anymore. Please take the gloves off of me." I beg this of everyone I see.
- The doctor is mixing different powders with water from the river and trying to inject it into my hands.
- James can't look at me.
- Each breath hurts as I feel the oxygenated blood going to my hands and bringing a fresh wave of pain with it.
- I search desperately for a machete or knife to cut my hands off with, but I can't close my hands around anything.
- I yell at the doctor, "You can't inject river water into me! I'll die!"
- I'm running faster than I've ever run before, as the pain dissipates if I outrun it.
- The crew tackles me as I run past them, holds me down, and tells me I can't run anymore.
- The ants are crawling up my boots, getting closer, and there are a few on my hands.
- There is no position I can put my hands in – a light breeze hits them and it feels like a wave of molten lava.
- I can't scream or cry.
- I start trying to tackle, bite, and headbutt the crew.
- Sol holds me with my head on her shoulder while I scream.
- I beg the doctor to make this stop.
- My muscles are twitching and going into spasm.

- The doctor says he can't find a vein, then injects something that looks like dishwater into my hand and arm. It does nothing for the pain but the hallucinations get worse.
- The river is rising, the ants are in the water.
- The ants are covering the bar that I rested my arms on and crawling all over the tent.
- The tribe is laughing at me because I screamed, horrible laughs, in my face, pointing their fingers at me and laughing.
- I beg James to cut my hands off.
- I think I will die if I don't cut my hands off.
- I'm screaming as James walks with me, holding me up, there is a rolled-up ace bandage in my mouth and my arm is dripping blood.
- I place my hands in a bucket of ice and I feel instant relief. Reality comes back.

Here is what the crew tells me really happened. They said it was one of the most traumatic things they have ever seen. After the dance ended, I spent about an hour walking up to each of them and asking them to take the gloves off. Then I warned Ben not to go into the hut because there were ants everywhere. (There were not – immediately after the ceremony, the inner gloves were shaken out of the outer ones, and chickens ate all of the ants.) I headbutted James, Ben, and Brendan. I hugged Sol and she held me while I yelled. I tried to bite Ben and they put a roll of gauze in my mouth, which I spat out. Ben apologized and brought me back into the hut to get some pictures, but I freaked out saying there were ants everywhere and screamed at him not to touch them. No one else was in the hut. I screamed over and over, then ran at full speed all over the village. I almost fell in a well but somehow jumped over it without looking down.

The doctor made the crew tackle me and stop me from running because he said increasing my heartrate like that could send me into shock, or I could fall in the well. I kept saying that it felt like my hands had been crushed, like each nerve was exposed. I begged them to take the gloves off and they told me that I hadn't been wearing the gloves for quite a while. I begged them to cut my hands off, then just started repeating "please, please, please, please," over and over for about half an hour. Then I started screaming again, jumped to my feet (I had been laying on my back, hands and feet in the air like a turtle) and tried to run. The entire crew held me back, everyone holding on, and I was still running through them, like a running back trying to shake off an entire line of defensemen. I pushed my head and shoulders into them, stamped my legs, screamed, and pushed them all back about 10 feet before collapsing.

I laid on the ground, breathing heavy. In a rare moment of clarity, I asked the doctor to please make this stop. The doctor tried to give me an injection but couldn't find a vein. I started screaming at him not to inject me with dirty water, and he put a hand on my shoulder to calm me. Finally, he injected a strong painkiller into the back of my hand while Ben poured in a mouthful of pills and Sol dumped some water in and forced me to swallow by rubbing my throat. They put an ace bandage in my mouth because I was clenching my jaw so tight that they thought I'd damage my teeth, and James then led me back to the boat. I screamed so loud that I went hoarse.

They said the other initiates acted much the same, minus the running – that was unique to me, I guess. No one laughed at me. In fact, village life basically went back to normal after the ceremony. Each initiate had a few handlers who stayed with them and made sure they didn't do anything stupid like cut their hands off or run into the river, but otherwise this was just another day in the Sateré-Mawé village.

After I got on the boat, the doctor put my hands in ice water and I started crying because it felt so good and my mind cleared so quickly. It was the best feeling I have ever had in my life. It was pure ecstasy. I started sobbing and crying uncontrollably because of how good it felt, and probably all of the drugs the shirtless doctor gave me kicked in around then.

The other initiates were led onto the boat and were in rough shape, even the would-be-chief. I invited them to share the ice, and when they put their hands in they cried too, saying how amazing it was. It's not considered the best form to do anything to dull the pain after the ceremony, but it's also not forbidden. Generally, the initiates are expected to deal with the pain for 4–5 hours, about when it peaks, and then they can try to numb it. Most get blind drunk. With our hands in the cooler, we started laughing. As soon as I took out my hands, even for a second, the pain flooded back in full force. The other initiates called me their brother now, hugged me, kissed my head and shook their heads at our bizarre shared experience. We were brothers in pain. After two hours of ice, I received more drugs and started to feel like myself.

The pain had plateaued. My hands still ached, a horrible, throbbing, dull pain even in the ice, but were pure agony out of it. The doctor, smoking as he examined my hands, said he was worried about frostbite. He asked me to do one minute in and five minutes out for the next hour. I barely managed this, and by the end of each five-minute stretch the hallucinations were kicking back in. Ten hours after the ceremony and the pain was as bad as it had been at its worst, and I was starting to have flashbacks to the ceremony.

The crew locked me in a room and opened the door periodically to refill the cooler and check that I was following the doctor's instructions about using the ice less. Our guide from a local tribe gave me acupuncture in my ear, arm, and hand and it seemed to help for about an hour, then the pain came back. He also gave me a massage, which helped with the muscle spasms that had started about six hours after the ceremony.

After 16 hours the doctor said he had to take the ice away as there was a good chance I would do permanent damage if I kept using it. I hadn't slept for a minute, and the pain wasn't at all diminished.

I could at least maintain consciousness by this time, so I decided to call Anna on our satellite phone and tell her I had survived. I walked out of the room to where the crew was gathered outside, and they all clapped and hugged me. They said how proud they were of me and started to tell some stories, but could see I was still hurting pretty bad, so they gave me the satellite phone and dispersed so I could talk to Anna. I caught a glimpse of myself in a mirror – I was midnight blue in weird streaks – my face, head, neck, chest, pants, legs, everywhere. There were hand marks on my back and stomach, streaks of skin color in the blue where sweat had pooled, and my hands were massive and swollen. The doctor appeared and said the swelling was probably from the drugs, but might have been from the stings, or the ice – he wasn't sure. They were at least double their normal size – my fingers looked like over-cooked blue sausages, and my knuckles had inverted. I clumsily pulled out my iPhone and took a couple of pictures of them. The pain was getting excruciating so I figured I needed to call before I lost the ability to speak again.

Dialing was no easy task, and if it hadn't hurt so badly I would have found it funny. Anna picked up after three or four rings. I had no idea what time it was in Boston, or in Brazil, for that matter.

She sounded groggy. "Hello?"

"Hey there, how are you?"

"How am I? I'm fine! Are you nervous? It's tomorrow if you do it, right?" I had forgotten the schedule changed after we'd arrived. Anna had the old itinerary.

"Actually, it was yesterday. Well, maybe 18 hours ago or so. I did it." Silence…

"You did? You did it? Oh my God! Congratulations! Good

for you. That is awesome. I can't *believe* that you did it! How do you feel? I'm really proud of you, ya know. You're insane."

I laughed for the first time in what felt like a really long time, and then gave her the highlights. I told her I was blue, about collecting the ants, Bret, the pain, hallucinations, etc. I told her, "Wait until you see the footage, it should be amazing." She said she couldn't wait, and then we hung up.

Ben tentatively asked if we could film a little bit, and I gave a bizarre, rambling interview. He determined that I was in no shape for coherent thought and called the doctor in. I was given more pills and another injection, which turned out to be a massive dose of painkillers and sleeping pills. I woke up and found that 25 hours had passed since the ceremony. My right hand felt okay – I could move it at least – but my left hand was still on fire, although it was a dull fire compared to the day before.

I finished the interview we had started before my drug-induced nap. James snapped a bunch of publicity shots, and I started joking around with the crew. I asked Ben if he ended up doing a sting, and he said that once he saw me hallucinating, he decided it wasn't a good idea: "For the show, you know? You can't have the producer running around tripping balls. Someone has to steer this ship. Of course, I'd have done it otherwise." We all laughed. James and Brendan teased Sol about crying until she told them to shut up and called them out for doing the same. They all told me how hard it was to see me in that much pain. Brendan kept saying he'd never forget it. I also found out we had moved about five miles downriver while I was locked in the room because there had been "an incident"…

One of the initiates had burned down a villager's hut after getting caught with the man's wife. A huge brawl had broken out. Another had snuck onto our boat with a machete, intent on killing us because, "We were witches who had caused this Tucandeira to be worse than any other." Our guide had tackled him, taken the machete, and walked him back to the chief, who just shrugged and said to Sol, "Sorry. Sometimes this happens. They lose their mind. How is yours?", referring to me. Sol told him I had lost my mind too. The only initiate with no story to tell the next day was the newest hunter, who never had to do this again. Our crew had decided to move the boat as a precaution, but no one had slept well.

We went back to the village and the chief looked at my hands. He turned them over, inspected them, then clapped them between his and smiled – kindly – at my grimace. He said, "Yes, this is good. You are now one of us," and patted my hands gently. He told me that the forest was open to me, and I would be welcomed back anytime I wanted to return. He said everyone, not just the Sateré-Mawé, would recognize me from the blue paint, and know that I was one of them. I hadn't realized this would be the case – I knew all groups of Sateré-Mawé would recognize the fact that I'd participated in the ritual and possibly share more of their legends with me, but I hadn't realized up until that point that other tribes might recognize me as Sateré-Mawé now. This ended up being an incredible boon when we visited the Karitiana tribe.

I thanked him profusely and said I was excited to speak with him and others in the tribe about their traditions. He smiled and told me to rest for now, which I did. But not before meeting Bret one final time. As he approached, I assumed he was there to make more unpleasant comments, or make fun of me, or tell me what a wuss I was for only doing it once – but, surprising everyone in our crew, he just nodded at me, smiled, shook my hand – then turned and walked away. The handshake wasn't overly aggressive, or light – it was a firm shake which hurt like Hell – but I could tell wasn't intended to make me grimace – and I didn't. It meant a lot to me – it meant I really was accepted.

Forty-two hours after the ceremony my hands still hurt – a dull, throbbing pain. The doctor said it could be because of the ice. I was losing a lot of skin on them and he was worried some rot might have set in from being wet for so long. He told me that what I had done was really stupid, then he hugged me, slapped my face, and laughed. He shook my hands and congratulated me. He was a weird dude.

I'd be blue for another two weeks, and the crew started calling me Avatar Pat or Nerdy Smurf. True to the tribe's word, their traditions, stories, and culture and the forest were opened to me. We spent just a couple of short days with them before heading to different villages and different spots in Brazil. The chief was right, the dye did the job. Everyone gave me immediate respect once I confirmed that I was blue from the Tucandeira. Even the tribes that didn't practice this ritual knew of it, and respected anyone who had done it. They trusted me immediately and asked to hear my stories as well as sharing their own. By the time we reached cities the color was fading. One woman at the airport asked Sol why her friend was blue. Sol replied, "Oh, he's from Boston," and the woman nodded, agreeing that this made sense.

Ben was right – it's the scene that everyone talks about and remembers. I continue to get questions about it. Icon did an amazing job of editing 42 hours of my agony into an extremely engaging eight-minute segment. My mom can't watch it. She cried when I finally told her about the bullet ants, months after doing it, and can't watch more than the tester sting.

Before the series aired, Anna and I had her cousins, my best friend Adam and my brother Nate over on Thanksgiving for our annual drunken holiday celebration. We were drinking a fair amount and they were pressing me about the show. I let a little slip about the bullet ants and they pounced on it, asking if I had any footage. I said I only had raw footage, nothing edited. They asked to see a little, teasing me, "I want to see you acting like a baby 'oh it stung me, oh it hurts so bad,'" etc., just having fun. Anna hadn't seen it yet and was as anxious as the others. We were all laughing and finally, after another terrible mixed drink (I was trying to recreate a drink Ben's partner had taught me and failing miserably, but it had a lot of alcohol), I agreed to show them a little bit. They saw I was shirtless as I started queuing up on one of the scenes on our iMac and started teasing me about how dirty and out of shape I looked. I hadn't told them about the mites, the dye, or anything else. We were laughing and I was saying how good the food was in Brazil, and how I couldn't help gaining a little weight while I was there.

Then I hit play.

The first thing I showed them was the gloves coming off. There was silence. No one said anything. I fast-forwarded to about 45 minutes after the ceremony when I was begging to take the gloves off. Adam looked away; Anna and her cousin were crying silently; Nate stared in horror. I fast-forwarded a little more and showed them me laying on the ground and screaming. Anna started sobbing and hit me, turning away. Nate said, in serious tones, "You can't let Mom see this. Seriously, you have to warn her not to watch." I had thought it was funny, but then I had seen it a bunch of times, plus I'd been through it. Adam asked me to turn it off. Anna just said it was really hard to see me in that much pain. After the initial shock, and a few years between then and now, they all joke about it. But that initial reaction was my first time seeing my loved ones' reaction to this, and it wasn't funny.

I will never forget the experience, and I believe most people who watch it won't either. In the end, it was one of the most absurd things I have ever done, but I am glad I did it. I'm equally glad that I will not do it 19 more times. It did what I intended it to – it showed the tribe that I respect their customs, and they honored me by telling me their legends and accepting me as one of their own. The experience changed me, forever. It's something I'll carry with me for the rest of my life.

I think back about the entire ordeal often. At first, when watching the footage, I would uncontrollably flex my hands. I didn't realize I was doing this until Barny pointed it out. I was traumatized and had a touch of PTSD. I saw some bullet ants going about their business a few days after the ceremony on a trek through the jungle and freaked out for a couple of minutes – hyperventilating and sweating. Throughout the rest of the trip in Brazil, whenever I saw some, I would force myself to pick one up on a stick and play with it for a little while to help overcome the fear I'd developed.

Thinking back on it now, I have a hard time pinpointing the true reason I did the ceremony. Yes, it was to gain the trust of the tribe, but it was much more than that. It was a once-in-a-lifetime experience. I couldn't pass up the opportunity. It's a story I'll be able to tell for the rest of my life, and something that truly sets me apart from most people. Yes, I'm okay admitting now that part of it was ego – the desire to have the best story at a party. And part of it was the desire to make the best series I possibly could. I love Icon, and a huge part of me wanted to do it to show them what *I* could do, how far *I* would go for them, for Nat Geo, and for our project. I knew this would set the series apart from other crypto and wildlife shows. As Ben said, I knew it would be, "the scene that everyone talked about." I knew the series would be great without it, but with it, it would be incredible.

The goading from Bret was a huge motivator, also. I'll admit that, without his obnoxiousness, I probably would have backed out. That tester sting was so intense, so mind-meltingly horrible, that I probably would have thrown in the towel and figured one sting was still pretty good had it not been for his derisive laughter and joy at seeing me back down. One sting would have been good for the show, a good story for me, and might have even gotten me a few points with the tribe. As unbearable as Bret was at the time, I have to admit I'm glad he was there. Not to compare myself to Buddha, but he was my demon Mara – provoking me to do what turned out to be the right thing, and I'm grateful to him.

I also feel bad for depicting him as a "Bret." In the intervening years I've had a lot of opportunities to reflect on the entire experience, and I've spent a fair amount of time trying to look at this from his perspective, and I have to say that Pat Spain does not look great through his eyes. I *am* a Westerner, an outsider, who clearly lives a comparatively privileged life. I came into his village, *his* village – the village he worked so hard for every day, the village he pushed himself to do the ceremony not once, not even twenty times, but close to thirty times in order to be a leader and help his tribe. I come in there and expect to be treated with respect? Why, because I'm on TV? The village doesn't have one TV – or electricity for that matter. Why should anyone care that I'm on TV. Worse still, everyone *did* seem to immediately like and respect me. The chief was willing to let me participate in their most sacred ritual – the most important part of their lives, and the most important accomplishment of this young man's life. I was given the opportunity to do it, even though no one seemed to think I would go through with it. Why should I be given the chance? Why should this Westerner be able to do this, like a stunt – with his doctor, medivac, camera crew, houseboat, and tester sting? It was bullshit in his eyes, and he wasn't shy about letting us know it. I see that now, and it hurts that I didn't see it or address it at the time.

Of course, this wasn't my intention. It wasn't a stunt to me, I was doing it to show respect, to show the world their amazing culture, to gain their respect and share an experience with them. The chief saw this opportunity to show others their world. The other initiates and tribe members saw this also, but I should not necessarily have expected this young hunter I've been calling "Bret" to do the same. I regret not seeing this at the time, but if I'd been more mature and recognized this I might not have gone through with it, because his goading was genuinely the final push that got those gloves on my hands.

A huge part of my motivation went beyond gaining the trust of the tribe, showing them respect, my own ego, my intense desire to show Icon what I could do, and shoving it in the face of this guy I had a misconception of. The biggest motivation was my own unguarded fascination at the opportunity to see the world from a different perspective. Not like what traveling does for you. Traveling to India, the Congo, etc., seeing intense poverty, having your eyes opened to the way so many in the world live *does* change you. But you are always still yourself while you're experiencing it. You take it in and process it based on your own experiences, knowing you can go back to your own life. I imagine that it's how Thoreau felt living a simple life on Walden Pond – he knew he could always leave and go back to the outside world as a fairly wealthy, Harvard-educated man. This doesn't take away from what must have been a transcendental experience, but it is always in the back of your mind – the "real" world, your world, is waiting for you. I wanted to momentarily live in a world where donning a pair of gloves filled with bullet ants was a normal thing to do.

Of all the rituals I've participated in, all of the meals I've shared, all of the places I've slept and the people I've spent time with, nothing other than the bullet ants truly showed me what it was to *be* a different person in a completely different world from the one I knew. I was hoping that the bullet ants would show the tribe I wasn't an outsider, but before doing it I didn't consider that it also meant not experiencing it as an outsider. I didn't consider what it would mean mentally to have the world you know disappear and be replaced with something "other." To actually have an experience living in "their" world – our world to a very small degree now, I guess, because my world *is* different now, and I certainly have seen the existence of "their" world. I am fully aware of it. Certainly, the ceremony changed my world, and forever after. It was actually surreal going back to Western civilization after the ceremony – knowing what I could put my body through and survive, but also that I wouldn't need this newly discovered knowledge. I had done this unthinkable ritual, put my body through more pain and emotional anguish than anyone could expect to survive, and then – I would work a desk job? My old world didn't make sense for a long time. I had no use for this incredible new enlightenment until I was diagnosed with cancer.

I recently got my first tattoo. A bullet ant, designed and inked by the amazingly talented Dia Moeller, who also illustrated the gorgeous covers for all of the *On the Hunt* series books. When I was going through chemotherapy, I had to have a port-a-cath implanted in my chest, which left a good scar – one of many from my entire cancer experience. I don't mind scars – in fact, I'm proud of all of mine – but I wanted to incorporate this scar with a tattoo.

Chemo was truly my personal Tucandeira, and hopefully the only time I have to draw on the new world I discovered within myself during the ritual in the Amazon. The initiates in the tribe had to walk up to that bar and place their forearms on it, knowing what was ahead of them, knowing the agony that would follow. They had to do this twenty times, of their own free will. They did it to provide a better life for themselves, their future families and their tribe. I had to walk into that hospital every two weeks for six months, step up to the chemo-chair, and have a needle stuck in my chest and poison injected into me, knowing what would happen, how horrible I would feel, how I would question whether I could survive it, anticipating the nausea and weakness and mental anguish. Knowing I'd be curled up in the fetal position for a day or more, or laying on the floor of the bathroom after vomiting and being too weak to stand up, or wearing gloves and wool socks in the summer because of the neuropathy caused by the poison injected into my heart, just as these initiates had poison injected into their hands.

I had to draw on the knowledge that my body could take this. I could survive it if I willed myself to. I drew on that knowledge whenever chemo was overwhelming and I felt like I couldn't do it again. I did it every two weeks. I would get the next dose just as I was starting to feel "normal" again, just like the initiates in the tribe. I did this to ensure a life for myself and my future family, and because I *knew* my body could handle it. In my new world, the blended world of the Mawé and a Bostonian, this was okay, normal. It didn't need to disrupt my life. I could work. I could drive myself to chemo. I could go through it and come out the other side healthy and stronger. I worked with Dia to place the tattoo in conjunction with the port scar, not covering it up, but touching it – complementing it, acknowledging that, in my mind, the bullet ants and chemo are the same.

Chapter 2

Is It Cool That I Just Boarded a Plane with a Propane Tank, Two Lighters, Several Knives and a Full-Size Bow and Arrow in My Carry-On?

There are very few things in this world that really set me on edge. I love horror movies, it's nearly impossible to embarrass me, public speaking is a major part of all of my job descriptions, and I naturally gravitate towards acts of stupidity that make others flinch. But if you want to see me squirm in fear your best bet is to either hit on me or have a stern individual in a uniform ask me a question. Any question and uniform will do – police, military, border patrol, even a flight attendant – someone who outwardly displays a tiny modicum of authority over some aspect of my life based simply on their occupation and I become a confused, jumbled, blabbering mess. The same is true if you hit on me. If a cop were to hit on me after pulling me over, I think I would enter a fugue state and ram their parked cruiser in a severely misappropriated "fight or flight" response.

There are many potential reasons for this, none of which would be interesting to anyone other than me, so I'll just state it as a fact. With this in mind, it should come as no surprise that I do not deal well with airports. Airports are filled with people in uniforms – people who have complete control over whether I make it to my intended destination and love to remind me of this superpower. I love traveling, but I hate airports. First, you encounter a police officer whose sole purpose is to prevent you from saying goodbye to the person who has dropped you off at the airport. If it's a loved one there is no kiss goodbye like in the movies, there's just an angry, red-faced officer screaming at you and blaring his siren, instructing you to "move your ass or get a ticket." If it's a cabbie it's impossible to even pay them without a threat of imprisonment if you haven't fished your card out long before stopping. There is no long, meaningful look into your dad's eyes as you embark on a great adventure, just a hurried, "What the hell is that guy's problem? Call your mother from the [police siren noise]... Jesus! Really? Fine, I'm going! Call your mother."

Next, you encounter a uniformed airline employee at the check-in desk who tries to argue that your bag is too large, or your carry-on cannot be carried on, or asks, in an accusatory way – as if already knowing the answer or somehow blaming the airline's policy of overbooking on you – if you'll switch flights with the grandmotherly older woman standing next to you, knitting, who's trying to get to her only grandchild's wedding. You give up all but one tiny bag which was previously in your intended carry-on, pay 14 hitherto-unmentioned fees, and, apologizing profusely, refuse to switch tickets. Then, feeling like an asshole, you slink to the security line while the old woman looks at you in shock and disgust and murmurs something to the judgmental ticket counter about there being "gentlemen in my day." While making your way down the line you encounter no less than 18 uniformed TSA agents, all of whom scribble something unintelligible on your ticket. Some of them feel you up while they breathe their stale-coffee and tater-tots breath on you and try not to look you in the eye while fondling you. Then you're instructed to take off nearly all of your clothing and attempt to stow it in the doll-sized carry-on you were allowed to keep with you, after you completely undo your careful packing job to remove your laptop and place it in a separate bin.

You walk, barefoot, through a bizarre array of scanning devices, lifting your arms when instructed, standing on the yellow feet marks when instructed, walking forward when instructed, stopping and waiting when instructed, opening your bags when instructed, and finally – if you are lucky and every member of the TSA has agreed that you do not pose a serious threat to the airplane you are hoping to board at some future point – you are allowed to repack your now lumpy and disarranged tiny bag, put your clothes and shoes back on, start to process the borderline sexual misconduct you've just experienced, and get in another line where an airline representative will ask to see yet another form of ID and tell you that the one carry-on you've managed to keep with you will have to be checked through to your final destination because they are overbooked and all overhead space is gone – taken up by a family of six who have managed to each bring four carry-ons and multiple strollers on the plane. That is *if* everything goes well. If you happen to rub any one of those 38 people up the wrong way, they can, and will, tie you up until you miss your flight, get arrested, or simply lose your mind.

Each time I head to the airport, I try to tell myself I will be okay. I can get through security with no problems because I haven't done anything wrong. I don't have any liquids or explosive materials in my carry-on. I am not hiding any weapons anywhere on my person. I don't have any illicit substances crammed into an orifice. I am not harboring ill thoughts about our plane, the pilot, or the flight crew, and am thus not committing any thought crimes – which I am sure one of the many scanners causing a recurrence of cancer will detect. I am, in all ways, an easygoing, agreeable traveler who isn't concealing anything. Why, then, why oh God why, am I *always* the "random" check?

The first time this happened I was 23 and on my way to film *King of the Jungle 2*, my first TV series on Animal Planet. I was terrified, excited, and jumpy – not good adjectives for a traveler at an international airport. The first airline employee I encountered at Boston's Logan Airport glanced at my ticket, which I had just printed from the lone functional kiosk in a sea of 505 error screens, and frowned: "Oh, sorry, looks like you are going to be the random check today. Oh, I probably shouldn't have told you that, huh?" She was in her mid-twenties with short brown hair, lots of freckles, brilliantly white teeth, and looked very hipster despite the airline uniform. She was flirting with me and wearing a uniform, so already I was sweating and getting uncomfortable.

"What? Whose check?"

Yup. "Whose check?" was my question. When, on one visit, a very good-looking Spanish woman at a burrito place I used to pick up food from saw my driver's license, flashed me a huge smile and leaned far across the counter, making her low-cut shirt even lower cut, grabbed my outstretched hand and said, in a fantastic accent, "Spain? That is my country! You must love Spanish women, yes?"

To which I replied, "I'm Irish," then awkwardly turned and walked away, leaving my food on the counter, and regretting that I'd never be able to order burritos from there again.

Brooke, as it said on her airline name tag, looked a little taken aback. She was probably thinking that maybe she really shouldn't have warned me about the random check. "Nervous flyer?" She asked.

"Yes," I lied. "My girlfriend told me I should get here a lot earlier." For some reason, anytime someone flirts with me, even a little, I find the need to make my next statement include the phrase "my girlfriend" (now "my wife"), even if that statement is completely unnecessary or an obvious lie, as it was in this case. I was there over two hours early for a domestic flight.

She replied, "Earlier than this and you'd be so bored you'd have to grab a drink with me in the lounge!"

Oh God she was still doing it. "You… said… they're going to… check me?", I stammered.

She rolled her eyes a little. "They check everyone, this little

SSSS on your ticket means you are the lucky winner who'll get a little extra checking out. And not by me." She smiled, and blushed a little.

Completely ignoring the flirtatiousness, I stammered, "What does that mean? Do they think I did something wrong? Am I going to miss my flight?" I was sweating a little by this point.

"Hey man, don't worry about it. It's not a big deal. They randomly pick a bunch of people. Unless you've actually got something in your carry-on that you shouldn't, you'll be fine." She said this in a way that let me know she was no longer interested in flirting me with, or in talking to me at all. I left that line to enter the security screening line, a little more curious than nervous, actually. What was this going to be like? Was I going to be interrogated?

I approached the first TSA check point, driver's license and ticket held in front of me like shields, protection from the takedown I was anticipating. As the man in the blue uniform took them, I stupidly said, "I guess I'm a random check, huh?"

One thing I have learned in these encounters is the less you say, the better it will go. At this point, however, I didn't know that.

"Whaddya mean? *Should* you be the random check?" The former high-school football player-looking 30 years old said. "Do you have anything you shouldn't? Do we need to do extra screening?"

"Um, no, not at all. The girl at the ticket counter said the little SSSS on my ticket meant I was the random check."

"She shouldn't have told you that. Who was she? What did she look like?" He said as he clicked his shoulder mike, saying, "I need an added security screen at line 3."

"Um, I don't remember what she looked like."

"You know, it's a crime to lie to me. You're not protecting her."

"No, no, I don't remember. She was young, I think?"

Oh God, was she young? Was she even a she? Suddenly an image of a young blonde man in an airline uniform came into my head. Was that him? No, that was Leonardo DiCaprio from *Catch Me if You Can*.

"Sir, step over here, please. This agent will perform your extra screening."

"I'm on my way to be on TV," I said, for no apparent reason.

"Ohhhh Kaaayyyy, well, we're just going to check through your carry-on over here, if you'll follow me."

"I'm a biologist."

"Yup, please follow me."

The TSA agent asked me to open my bag and where I was on my way to, looking through my clothes with a wand while I blabbed out lengthy answers. He finally cut me off mid-sentence and said, "Why are you so nervous?"

Here's the shittiest thing about getting nervous around police, TSA, border guards, etc. – the more nervous you are, the more suspicious you look, and the question "why are you so nervous?" lets you know that, which in turn makes everything worse.

"Uh, I'm not?" I replied, as all the color drained from my face and I started sweating.

"Are these your shoes, sir?" he said, holding up the new pair of Chuck Taylor Allstars I bought for the taping. I had my friends and family sign them and write notes to me on them – they were my "personal item" – the thing every first wave US reality show played up. "Each contestant is allowed one personal item to make them feel more at home and express themselves." Chucks were the only shoes I had worn since third grade, and they had a special place in my heart – even if they had been the cause of knee surgery the year before.

"Yes," I replied, watching as he read them.

"What does this mean?" he asked, pointing at a message Anna had written on them. It was from Salinger's *Nine Stories*, one of my favorite books. The line was from Seymour and read: "If you want to look at my feet, say so, but don't be a God-damned sneak about it. I have two normal feet and can't see the slightest God-damned reason why anybody should stare at them."

"Um, it's from a book. Salinger, the guy who wrote *Catcher in the Rye*, and it's a turning point for the character of Seymour Glass. I really like that book, and my girlfriend wrote it on my shoe, and I always thought it meant that, you know, Seymour didn't want people to see where he had been – like when he came back from the..."

"Why is it written on your shoe? Do you not want me to look at your shoe? Is there anything about your shoe that you don't want people to see? This is not a normal thing to have written on a shoe. In fact, it isn't normal to write on a shoe at all."

"I've always written on the white part of my Chucks, I guess. It's a quote..."

"Yeah, you said that. Maybe there's more to this shoe?"

"No, it's just a shoe."

"With a quote on it that says not to look at it, because it's normal."

This might seem excessive now, but this was 2003, and the "Shoe Bomber" was still on the news pretty regularly. Looking back, having anything that drew attention to shoes probably wasn't the best idea when flying.

"Okay, please zip up your bag and follow me," he said evenly, as he walked toward another room, carrying my shoes.

"Why do I have to go in there?" I murmured, following.

"Is there any reason you wouldn't want to go in there?" he asked. "Any reason why you wouldn't want me to have a closer look at these?" he said, shaking my Chucks.

"Yes," I thought, "lots of reasons. Body cavity searches, no-fly lists, missing my flight, abuse of power, planting evidence, and body-cavity searches all jump to mind." Luckily, I was cognizant enough to simply say, "No."

We went to the most nondescript room in Logan Airport. It wasn't exactly white or gray, and didn't smell bad but it had a stale feeling, like it had been designed to bore you. The chairs were cheap plastic and the table was cheap MDF and laminate. The agent and I were the only ones in the room. He asked me to put my bag on the table.

"Why are you so nervous, buddy? You make me nervous if you're this nervous," he said, turning over my shoes, feeling them inside and out, pressing on the non-existent cushioning.

"I just don't do well in these situations. Not that I've been in these situations before. But I mean, if I get pulled over or if a cop stops me on the sidewalk, or even in school, if a teacher asked me a question out of the blue. I just kind of freeze and get nervous. I don't even like running into people I don't expect to see, even really good friends. If I don't know I'm going to see them and I run into them somewhere, I act really weird. I think I'm kind of an awkward guy, ya know? Kind of weird. I really like working with animals. I'm on my way to Florida to film a nature show for Animal Planet. I'm not supposed to tell anyone that, I had to sign a bunch of contracts, but I think it's okay if I tell you, right? Anyway, yeah, I'm just nervous that I'm going to miss my flight or something, and those shoes are just shoes with some writing on them. It's for the show – I had everyone sign them and write stuff to me. It's a little weird, but kind of funny, right? And the quote is from a book I really like and it doesn't mean anything about the flight. It's just, they're just shoes."

Wow.

"Um, okay, you're just kind of a nervous dude, huh?"

"Yes."

"Do you have anything in your bag that's making you nervous?"

"Definitely not."

"Are you sure?"

"Absolutely, I swear. There is nothing in my bag or my shoes that I shouldn't have on a flight. I put all of my camping supplies and all liquids in my checked bag. All I have is some clothes, some gum, a couple of books, and some new shoes with writing on them."

"Okay, you're all set. Don't get nervous next time, okay? And don't have weird shit written on your shoes," he said, handing them back to me.

"I'll try," I promised and as I took them, I reached out to shake his gloved hand. When I saw that I probably shouldn't have done that, I moved like I was going to give him a fist-bump, then turned it into an offered one-arm bro-hug. He, correctly, stepped back and eyed me.

"Just an awkward, nervous dude," he said, shaking his head and chuckling as he walked away.

I left the room hoping I would never have to repeat that experience. I made it to Florida and back with no further incidents. On my way to DC a few months later, though, I saw the same SSSS on my ticket. "What the Hell?" I said to the confused airline worker who handed me the ticket.

"Is there something wrong?" asked the uniformed ticket-counter worker.

"Yeah, I'm the 'random' check again?" I asked, emphasizing "random" with air quotes.

"I don't know, sir. We don't have any control over that."

"I'm sorry, I know. It's just – I don't like being the random check. I don't have anything I'm not supposed to. I just don't like it."

"No one does. Next please."

Okay, I wasn't going to let this ruin the flight. I was prepared for this. I was wearing as little as I possibly could without calling more attention to myself. I had on flip-flops, comfy blue cargo shorts that an old man in Boston had once stopped me on the street to tell me were "excessive" due to their length, and a green T-shirt advising you "Leaves of Three, Let it Be," with a drawing of poison ivy on it. I had no threatening materials or illicit substances anywhere on my person, or any banned literary references. Also, I was going to keep my mouth shut and do exactly what the TSA agents told me to do.

I took a few breaths, steadied myself, and walked to the first checkpoint. "Afternoon, sir, where are you heading?" asked a very disinterested TSA ticket checker.

"DC," I stated – proud of myself for leaving out, "visiting friends and meeting with Animal Planet. Also, I know I'm the random check and I'm ready for it," as I instinctually wanted to say.

"Looks like you've been tagged for additional screening. Don't worry, it's just a random check. Please step this way."

"Okay, no problem," I said, much more calmly than I felt, as I stepped a couple of paces out of line and was greeted by a bored looking but stern-faced, 40-something-year-old Hispanic man.

"So, Mike here is going to perform the check," said the first agent.

"Hello, Mike," I said, and received only a, "I don't give a shit about you, and don't call me 'Mike,'" look in return.

"This way, sir," Mike said, leading me over to a less-crowded luggage scanner. He cut the line and asked me to please proceed as I normally would – shoes, belts, anything metal, anything in my pockets in the bin, laptops out, etc.

"I don't have a laptop with me, and do flip-flops count?" I asked.

Mike rolled his eyes and repeated word for word what he had just said. "Please proceed as you normally would at this point – shoes, belts, anything metal, anything in your pockets in the bin, laptops out and in their own bin, coats or bulky outer garments in their own bin. No liquids or gels. All toiletries or small amounts of liquid in a clear plastic bag and out of your luggage." Okay, that was my one question – from here on out, I was going to do exactly what he said, no discussion.

I started taking everything out of my pockets and putting them in the bins. I put my flip-flops in there and took my belt off. It was then that I noticed something. My shorts were old – very old – and the button had fallen off about a year before. I was using a safety pin to keep them closed – a safety pin made of metal, that was sharp, and maybe a weapon? They were so big that I never unbuttoned them, so I hadn't noticed the pin when I put them on that morning. I removed it and placed it in the bin.

"Please step this way," said a once-again disinterested Mike as he pointed through a metal detector. I stepped through, holding my pants up with one hand.

"Please retrieve your personal belongings and bring them here."

I did as instructed, not even mentioning the safety pin, asking if it was okay or explaining why I had it. I was trying my best to not be "an awkward, nervous dude." Mike asked me to open my carry-on and if he had permission to look through it. I did as asked, and said simply "yes."

He then asked me to raise my hands to chest height and said he was going to scan my hands for bomb-making material. I nodded. As I lifted my hands, I could feel my pants opening up. I had stood with my legs far enough apart that I didn't think they would drop down to my ankles, but I hadn't counted on the zipper falling of its own volition. As Mike scanned my hands, it seemed like I could hear every tooth of the zipper as it dropped a little further, opening wider and wider. He finished with my hands and stated: "Please keep your hands there while I check your bag." I nodded. He started checking through my bag with a little plastic wand while I stood there, becoming more and more exposed.

My pants had opened enough that I could now feel the

cool air on places that normally don't feel a breeze in public. I realized with a sense of horror that not only was my zipper slowly dropping, but my boxers were also wide open, and if the zipper fell a little more *everything* would be hanging out. Mike had told me not to move my hands, however, so up they stayed while my zipper went down.

I glanced down and was horrified to see that what I feared would happen had come to pass. I was standing, stock still, with everything I've got just hanging out. I heard a loud "oh my!" and looked straight in front of me where two older ladies were staring, open mouthed, in my direction. I started mouthing, "Sorry! Sorry! Nothing I can do, I have to keep my hands up." They blushed, made a "my oh my" gesture, and gave me a thumbs up. I smiled a little, shrugged, and apologized once again, wordlessly, then waited for this to be over.

"Well, Mr. Spain," started Mike, turning away from my bag and back towards me "You are all – what the fuck?" He had glanced down.

"Can I please put my hands down?" I asked, slightly panicked.

"What is wrong with you? Fix yourself!" He yelled.

"Yes, sir. I'm sorry, sir, you told me to keep my hands up, and my button fell off and my zipper…"

"So you were just standing there like that, with your wiener out, the whole time?" he stammered, incredulously, cutting me off.

The fact that he had said "wiener" barely registered as amazing. "Not the whole time, just maybe the last 15 seconds. You told me not to move my hands, and once a guard told me not to move my hands and I did and he pulled a gun on me, so I just kept my hands up here. I'm sorry."

Mike cracked the first smile I'd seen on him "Wow. Okay, thank you for not moving your hands. But you also, you know, could have said something. Please put your belt back on and don't... just don't, okay?"

"Yes, sir, thank you, sir. Can I board the plane?"

"Yes, please leave," said Mike, but I could tell he was suppressing a smile, and I knew I had given him a good story to share at dinner that night. I walked away, but not before I glanced back at the old ladies and yelled, "Sorry!"

"Don't be!" they yelled back, and laughed.

After that experience I have become accustomed to being the random check, and have switched to boxer-briefs. (I assume Mike put me on some flasher watchlist, or at least some permanent "always make this guy go through additional screening" list.) It happens 4 out of 5 times I fly domestically. Anna won't go in the same line as me anymore for fear that she will somehow become a known associate and end up on the same list. I know that each time I step into that line, whether there are 4 Ss on my ticket or not, I am most likely going to end up in a small, stale, grayish room with cheap furniture, or at least felt up by no less than three TSA agents. I've made my peace with it.

This has occasionally spilled over to international travel as well. I've had the pleasure of becoming acquainted with German "extra screening" techniques, argued with Hong Kong officials about what is a knife and what is not, and been pulled into the "naughty room" in Abu Dhabi. All of this is to say – if you see me at an airport, walk in the other direction, but don't run, because that will draw attention to you. One would think that all of these experiences would make me more used to being singled out, and I should know how to handle it now. You would be wrong. I still get the same nervous pit in my stomach, still ramble and sweat, and still make the same mistakes in a Sisyphean cycle. I have managed to refrain from attempting to hug TSA agents, but otherwise each interaction is as if I was back in that room in Logan in 2003.

It should be no surprise therefore that the amount of air travel required for *Beast Hunter* caused some interesting interactions between our crew and the TSA. It didn't help that we also played the "how much of a discount can we get on our luggage" game. This was done through flirtation, which rarely ever worked, claiming ignorance by pretending to be flustered with all of the paperwork, hoping someone would take pity on us and waive the fees rather than explain them for the thirtieth time to the confused foreigners, which worked even less frequently than flirting, or going with an "information overload" technique. This involved bombarding a poor airline worker with extraneous forms, attempts to pay in multiple currencies, adding and removing bags seemingly at random, and dropping rapid-fire, confident declarations like, "Gilang over in check-in said we wouldn't have to pay for this bag because it falls under the international agreement between Great Britain and your country." The hope was that the person would want to avoid losing face and just waive all fees rather than wade through everything we were presenting. The risk, though, was that they would get angry at the feeling of inadequacy we had fostered in them and make us all terror suspects.

In Indonesia, at the Soekarno-Hatta International Airport, James's flirtations were met with suspicion. I was behind him in line and laughed to myself as the young woman he was complimenting cut him off and said, "I must check you for bombs. Now."

James, always at ease in any situation, simply smiled and said, "Yeah, okay."

The woman started prepping a small device that looked like a Geiger counter. As she was putting a circular disc into the wand portion, James held his hands out – we had all been scanned at some point in our travels and knew the drill. "No," she said. "Please put your hands in the pockets of your coat."

James did as he was told.

"Please move them in your pockets, like you are searching for keys."

"Alright, sure," said James as he moved his hands around, smiling impishly.

"Now please remove them."

James held his hands out.

"No!" she stated more firmly and loudly. "Put them in the pockets of your jeans."

By this point, a crowd that included Barny (series producer), Simon (camera for Sumatra), and I were gathered around watching James, all of us having miraculously made it through security with no issues, but paying the additional baggage fees. Each command seemed to be getting progressively louder.

"Yeah, okay, here we go," said a smirking James while he put his hands in his pockets with cartoonishly exaggerated movements. He even rocked back and forth a little and whistled, doing a good Huck Finn impression, then removed his hands.

"No, keep them in your pockets now!"

"What?" said a still smiling but starting to get concerned James. "Ohh kaay."

"Please move your hands around."

James complied, blushing a bit and commenting "I think I need an adult – this is getting weird man." And made an exaggerated sad face while awkwardly fiddling around in his jeans pockets.

"Rub your hands back and forth, vigorously," was her next directive, which elicited a collective chuckle from the gathered onlookers.

"Rub my hands vigorously in my pockets? C'mon, you're joking?"

She didn't reply – just stared at him. Laughing nervously and very confused now, James started rubbing his hands along his thighs inside his pockets – aggressively. It was embarrassing to watch. He was getting red faced from the exertion and was only breaking direct eye contact with her to give some pleading looks our way.

"That's enough," the non-smiling woman said. "Stop now." A sheepish, heavy-breathing, and red-faced James removed his hands from his pockets and, cowed, held them for inspection without making further eye contact.

She scanned his hands and told him he was clear, after he paid all of the extra baggage fees and more.

In Brazil, after the bullet-ant ceremony, I was in no shape to attempt any sort of bargaining with airlines. In fact, I could barely even carry my own bags. I was still pretty out of it a couple of days after the ceremony as we prepped to board a flight to a different location in the Amazon. James and Sol helped as much as they could with my luggage (which had only arrived the day before). I wasn't really focused on what materials had made it into what bags as we entered the airport and got in line. I was distracted by the throbbing pain in my hands, the fact that my entire upper body was dyed navy blue, the intensely itchy rash covering my stomach and chest that indicated the chicken mites living in there were still alive and well, and the floating feeling in my head from the drugs our sketchy doctor had given me that morning before departing in a cloud of cigarette smoke. I had only recently regained the ability to have a full conversation.

Ben asked if I had everything and I looked at James, who looked at Sol, who gave the thumbs up. "I didn't go through your personal bag, Pat," Sol said, "but I made sure your luggage was all set. I'll help you getting it onto the belt."

"Thanks, Sol, you're awesome," I mumbled, smiling.

"Do you want me to take your carry-on?" asked Ben, still feeling guilty about his role in the bullet-ant experience.

"No, I'm good. I've got it, thanks," I lied.

"Actually, we've all got to take one or two of these other bags as well, to save on the fees," James said. "Ben, you've got the camera and your bag, so you take the small one. Sol, here are two for you. Ben, here are two for you. Pat, are you happy to take this one?" James asked, holding a small canvas bag. "It has a lot of random wires and batteries and whatnot in it, so if they ask anything just tell them it's camera equipment, and if they need to see any paperwork direct them to me, yeah?"

"What? Yeah, okay, no worries, I've got it. Can you sling it over my arm?" I said, groggily.

"Sure, mate. Here we go," and with that I had my second carry-on and was ready to get in line.

This was a rural airport in the middle of the Amazon, but flying is flying, and there were still about a dozen people checking our tickets, asking our intentions in going where we were going, etc. Our paperwork was scrupulously inspected, our medical records doublechecked to ensure we were not introducing disease to the indigenous populations we'd be visiting, and my appearance was asked about more than once. The fact that I'd performed the Tucandeira wasn't lost on most people in the airport (the blue skin gave me away), many of whom asked to see my hands then gave me the thumbs up, shaking their heads, impressed.

We finally reached the scanner where you put your bags on the conveyor belt and they pass through an X-ray. As we waited on the other side to collect them, I realized I had left a lighter in my bag, and quietly turned to Brendan.

"Hey, Brendan, there's a lighter in my bag. Think they'll notice?"

"I dunno, man, these rural airports can go either way – they're either super lax on security or very strict. Let's hope this one is lax."

"Should I tell them? Should I say something? Isn't it better to say something before you get caught?"

"Nah, relax, Pat. Just relax, don't worry. Worst case, they throw it away."

"Shit, I probably shouldn't have brought that bow and arrow either, huh?"

I had received a bamboo bow and quiver of arrows from one of the tribes we had been with and, in a stupor, had wrapped it in an old pizza box with Duct Tape around it, then attached it to my carry-on.

"It's in your luggage, right?" asked a now slightly concerned Brendan.

"No, fuck, I forgot. I didn't want it to get smashed, so I kept it in my carry-on."

"In that pizza box?" asked Brendan, laughing. "There aren't any poison tips on the arrows or anything, right?"

"I... don't think so?" I said. "Shit, that was really dumb, huh?"

"Not the smartest, but wait and see what happens. It's a traditional bow and arrow, not something that could take down a person. The tips aren't even stone, they're bamboo. It's probably fine."

"You think? Really?"

"No, but we'll see," said a grinning Brendan.

I started sweating, and my anxiety was rising with each passing minute that we didn't have our luggage. Finally, after what felt like half an hour, it came out the other side – my pizza-box still intact.

"See, all set!" said Brendan. "Let's go."

I smiled, asked him to load the bags into my arms, and boarded. Ben and James gave me a hard time for bringing weapons on the flight and we were all laughing when we landed a short while later. As we waited for our checked bags, I opened my carry-on and was horrified to see not only the lighter I remembered, but also a second larger one, as well as a canister of propane. I nudged James and showed him.

"Holy shit, mate! How did we miss that?" he asked. And that wasn't all. In the bag James had given me there was a small container with a camping knife in it. James was laughing hard by the time we found that, and he called over Ben and Sol. We dug further and found two more knives that I had forgotten about in my carry-on. One was a Gerber, with a good-sized locking blade, and the other a Leatherman multipurpose tool with a fair-sized knife and other stabby accoutrements. I then remembered the waterproof container holding camping matches in the front pocket.

Ben started laughing. "Wow, mate. With your bow and arrow that's basically everything you'd need to bring the plane down, huh? Good thing TV's Pat Spain is a peaceful sort of guy, isn't it?"

"There's no way that X-ray scanner was on at the airport, is there?" I asked.

"Either that or the bloke working it fell asleep. Either way, you're lucky," said James. "I'm pretty sure if this was America the full body cavity search would be well underway by now."

He was not wrong.

Chapter 3

Do All Luxury Hotels Have Jaguars?

There exists in many peoples' minds an image of a male wildlife-adventure TV host. Along with this image is a notion of where said host sleeps most nights while filming. These images generally fall into two camps — a rugged, scruffy, battle-scarred outdoorsman sleeping in a homemade lean-to, cooking a meal of the insects he'd just foraged, mixed with the blood of a rattlesnake and maybe some single malt that he brought in his hip flask for this occasion. Or, alternately, a camera-ready male-model-type, square-jawed, lithe, with stage makeup and hair product, who couldn't actually survive for a night without a team of handlers and who, once the camera goes off, stays in a luxury hotel.

I am certainly neither of those people — honestly, I don't believe any host is either of those people; not the ones I've met, at least. Yes, I love camping and do enjoy eating bugs — but no one would ever describe me as "rugged" or "lithe". I like a good whiskey now and then, but I prefer gin or cider. I'm also not embarrassed to say that I had oil-absorbing blotter paper in one of my bag's pockets and wore Spanx undershirts on most episodes of *Legend Hunter*. I'm also not embarrassed to say I went days, sometimes more, without bathing or washing my clothes on most shoots, and it didn't bother me one bit.

Likewise, our accommodations were not quite lean-tos, but I would not describe them as luxurious either. Most of the time, we were either camping in super-lite minimalist tents that could be set up and taken down easily, or in what could be described loosely as hotels, in that they were buildings with rooms that we could sleep in in exchange for money. Both required mosquito nets and silk cocoon-style sleeping sacs to keep bugs and diseases at bay.

For the Brazil shoot, I knew we'd be dividing our time between camping and "hotels", and I thought I knew what to expect from both. Camping would be tents set up in a semicircle for safety, on hard ground, dig a hole for the bathroom, etc. No frills, but fairly safe and standard. The hotels would likely have a musty odor and greasy, thin sheets, possibly a functional bathroom (either in each room, shared, or outside the hotel), unreliable electricity, a mattress that would be a toss-up if it were safe to sleep on, and a number of insect, small mammal, and reptilian friends to share the room with. The crew and I had developed our own 5-star rating system:

- 5 stars – Functioning air conditioning — automatic 5 stars, no matter what else was happening with the room or the hotel at large;
- 4 stars – Functioning shower, toilet, sink, warm water, and fan;
- 3 stars – Electricity available more than 50% of the time and an indoor bathroom;
- 2 stars – More spiders than other types of bugs, no rats;
- 1 star – Probably best to sleep on the floor and keep any food in airtight containers

Our accommodations in Brazil destroyed this rating system and spoiled me for all future travel shoots. I arrived at the Eduardo Gomes International Airport sans luggage, despite the Atlanta airline agent's assurance that it would arrive with me. My flight from Boston was delayed, which left me running at top speed through the Atlanta airport to make my connection. I arrived at the gate, panting, soaked with sweat, hobbling from a twisted ankle I'd gotten when attempting a complicated cut-fake-weave so as not to bowl over a 90-year-old Russian woman, and generally angry, only to be told that the plane door was closing, and if I could make it down the aisle before it closed, I would make the flight. "Once the door is closed, however, it can't be reopened," said the obnoxiously slow-talking Southern flight attendant. I limped-ran as fast as I could with my two carry-ons and just managed to get an arm through the plane door as the flight crew was closing it. They seemed surprised to see me but congratulated me on making it. I explained that I had luggage that was probably still being unloaded from my Boston flight and was told, patronizingly: "If you made it to this plane, I assure you that your luggage did too." This statement was accompanied by a huge "aren't you an idiot" grin from the inanely happy flight attendant. I believed him — there were just too many teeth in that grin not to trust it.

So, here I was, alone, in Brazil for the first time, with a "less than 10% battery" warning on my cell, two carry-ons, and the clothes on my back. Luckily, Brazil was the fifth shoot in the series, and I had gotten pretty good at packing the essentials in my carry-ons for just such a scenario. I had my filming uniform on, including a pair of stink-proof Exofficio boxer briefs (which could go 30 days without changing), wool socks, hiking boots, camo cargo pants, anti-malarial meds, and a paramilitary-style explorer shirt. I also had a solar charger and an outlet/voltage converter, a toothbrush, wildlife field guides for Amazonia, my camera, and lots of snacks. I did not have toothpaste, a change of clothes, any other footwear or socks, bug spray, sunblock, snake sticks, deodorant, toiletries, painkillers, anti-diarrhea meds, or anything for sleeping such as a camping pillow or sleep sack. Great start to the trip.

The crew was slated to meet me the next day at our hotel, and our fixer, Paulo, was supposed to be waiting for me at the airport. Much like my luggage, though, Paulo was nowhere to be seen. I was happy to find that, despite the low-battery warning on my cell, I actually had full bars. I placed a call to the lovely Anna at Icon, waking her, who told me to hang tight —

they would locate Paulo and my luggage and get them on their way to me momentarily.

I thanked her profusely and hung up, surveying my surroundings for the first time. It was then that I noticed that I was sweating copiously. It was around 11 p.m. and had to be 95º with close to 100% humidity. I saw a couple of middle-aged guys sitting on a bench with signs displaying people's names resting in their laps. They noticed me looking and held up the signs, hopeful I was their fare. I indicated that I was not but walked towards them anyway. The taller one was just over 50, overweight, very tan, with curly black hair and lively eyes. His pudgy hands were using a homemade sign that read "Gonzalez" as a fan, and he was sweating as much as I was.

The shorter one was skinny and looked to be about the same age. He had a mullet and all the indications that he was a lifelong smoker. His eyes looked a little jaundiced but crinkled into a mass of wrinkles when he smiled, and he invited me to sit down.

As soon as I did, the taller one with curly hair ventured, "American?"

"Yes," I said, "American. It's very hot tonight."

"Yes, very hot. Sticky. You need a ride? I don't think this guy is coming." He motioned to the "Gonzalez" sign he was holding.

"No, thank you, though. I'm waiting for someone who should be here soon."

"Okay, if you change your mind, let me know."

He had a nice voice, very smooth and warm. Both men then abruptly began an incredibly uncomfortable (for me) conversation about intimate details of their marriages and respective wives' anatomy, which, if they were to be believed, were cartoonish in proportions. There was no bragging or bravado here — it was like a conversation about cooking:

"My wife really makes the best meatloaf."

"Oh! That sounds so good right now! I wish we had some meatloaf."

"Yeah, she usually makes mashed potatoes with it too."

Except it wasn't about meatloaf; it was an extraordinarily detailed conversation about their sex lives. I am not a prude, but this took me by surprise. These guys apparently didn't even know each other, and they certainly didn't know me. Just as I was trying to figure out how to extricate myself from the situation, Paulo showed up, apologizing profusely and guiding me towards the customer service desk.

"Good-bye my friend! I hope you find many women to love in Brazil" Mullet said as I walked away.

"Oh, no, I have a girlfriend. Thank you, though," I yelled back.

"I'm so sorry!" shouted Curly, who was now fairly far away. "While we are both making love with our wives tonight, you will be missing your girlfriend a lot, huh?" he yelled loudly, in a very nearly empty airport.

"I guess so, yes?" I awkwardly replied.

"Looks like you made some friends." Paulo said, laughing.

He explained that the airline had told him earlier that day that I had missed the connection and would be on a flight tomorrow. "They have no record of you being in Brazil." He told me. I explained that they must have been thinking of my luggage, which was, to the best of the airline's knowledge, currently enjoying a stay in Texas. He went to the service desk to try and work out the details around when my luggage would be arriving, and how to get it to me once it was here.

While he was dealing with nightshift airline customer service at a small airport in Amazonia — a treat, I'm sure — he suggested I grab a bite to eat at the burger place around the corner. As I approached it, I was overly excited to find that it was called Bob's Burgers. I realized quickly that there was not going to be any Sweet Home Avocado Burger on the menu, however, because this was basically the Brazilian equivalent of McDonald's. After consuming the worst meal I would have in Brazil (which still wasn't bad by any means), we headed to the hotel.

As we approached, we passed several nightclubs with disco lights, thumping Latin drums, and scantily clad women shaking everything they had, both inside and outside the club. Paulo looked longingly at one club, Cabaret, and said, "This is a good place. I've had lots of fun here. So many fun nights. You should check it out tonight, yes? You are single?" I explained I had a girlfriend whom I lived with back in America. He sighed. "Ah, well, that is a shame. Brazil is for the single. Me? I have a wife who I love. But we have a new baby now. No dancing and nightclubs for a few months." Paulo told me to go out and have a Skol, the bestselling beer in Brazil. "The beer that goes down round," their slogan proclaims. This beer has gotten in a lot of trouble for sexually demeaning ads, which, based on other ads I saw there, must have been really demeaning to be called out. The slogan refers to round soccer balls and round body parts. Skol is also very popular in parts of Africa, and a Congolese MC with the amazing name of Bill Clinton Kalonji made a music video tribute to it featuring an inordinate amount of gyrating and yellow and green.

Paulo dropped me at the hotel and joked that he might stop at Cabaret on his way home, but probably not. I was staying at the Hotel Tropical — a sprawling complex that seemed to be a carryover from colonial expansion into the New World. My first impression was that it was beautiful, far beyond anything I had expected. It was striking — a grand marble and old, dark wood entrance opened to a massive dining area and bar, a staircase that had to be thirty feet across, mammoth exposed beams in the ceiling, incredibly ornate wood carvings on the walls, intricate patterns on the floor, and decorative columns everywhere. This had to be the wrong place.

I turned to walk back outside and let Paulo know he had dropped me at the wrong Hotel Tropical. There must be another place with the same name down some back alley reeking of urine, with a half-broken neon sign and a drug deal taking place in the parking lot. "Luxury" had never been part of the travel deal for me. Before *Beast Hunter*, any travel related to biology or filming meant I was paying for it, and that meant the cheapest option was the only option.

My first time living away from home was for a marine bio internship in southern Maine. I was 16, turning 17, and lived in an unlocked barn for six weeks. I loved every second of it — even the sound of mousetraps getting sprung in the middle of the night and cleaning up its consequences in the kitchen area in the morning. The signs reading "If it's yellow leave it mellow, if it's brown, flush it down" hanging on the semi-functional bathroom. The paper-thin walls that were often covered with beetles. The refrigerators whose shelves housed my veggie sandwiches nestled next to unbagged scientific specimens and chemicals used to preserve other specimens. Waking up with ticks burrowed into my belly button despite not leaving my room. I was only getting paid $50 a week, and that needed to cover all expenses, and the barn was free for any employees, so it was home. Yes, it was rustic — but it was science! And I genuinely loved it.

While filming *Nature Calls*, my self-written, funded, and produced YouTube-based wildlife-adventure series, I brought our crew to Arizona where we opted to camp rather than stay in the only place I could have afforded to put us up in near our filming location — the terrifyingly named "No-Tel Motel". The first night, Dom, our cameraman and one of my best friends, woke up completely covered in stinging ants after falling asleep on a picnic table, not realizing that he was covered in jelly. A jelly jar had broken in his luggage and he changed clothes in the dark before going to sleep. When the stinging woke him up, he also found a bark scorpion (the most dangerous scorpion in the US) a few inches from his bare leg. The next day, one of our cameras was stolen while Colin, another very close friend and cameraman, showered. We eventually tracked it down and confronted a sketchy couple in the nicest RV in the campground. They claimed to have "found it" in the public shower — in Colin's bag, under his clothes — while he was in the shower. We weren't going to argue and were just glad to have it back without having to fight anyone. That night, a man in the campsite next to ours blasted sad lost-love oldies from his truck, which he slept in the bed of with his two dogs. The third night we had to call 911 after hearing a loud domestic violence situation in our other neighbors' campsite, stepping in to intervene and protect a young, very drunk woman. I still think we made the right call and it was better than the No-Tel.

The next big Nature Calls adventure was to Costa Rica! My first international shoot and a country often associated with luxury travel. But we were once again being funded by the Bank of Spain (not unlike Columbus — but definitely unlike him in literally every other way) meaning I was maxing out credit cards left and right and we could barely afford to eat — so, instead of eco-resorts, we filmed army ants carrying crabs and small mammals up the walls of our hotels, and received electric shocks in the showers. Costa Rica was the first place I encountered an "on demand" water heating system. In some new construction in nice places, this is a great innovation! A small water tank rapidly heats the water you draw as you need it. Efficient! Not so in the places we were. This system was usually a jerry-rigged electrical contraption added to the showerhead that, when turned on, heated the water leaving the shower to a tepid "nearly room temperature". Turning it on often burned your fingers and gave you electric shocks and, since I was paying and booked these places, this became my job for most of the trip. To start the shower for everyone else.

In fact, in order to get my education in biology, I lived in less-than-ideal conditions. My first apartment in Boston was in Back Bay. If you're familiar with Boston, you're probably thinking, "Back Bay, wow; I wish I could afford that!" Well, guess what? You can. The only catch is that you have to live in a ground-floor back-alley apartment that is actually a two-car garage turned into two separate apartments — and by "separate" I mean separated by uninsulated drywall, of course. The other apartment was occupied by a minister who loudly "prayed" and sounded like he was whipping himself until after 1 a.m. each night. On the other side of the apartment was a crawlspace, which I incorrectly assumed was used for storage of maintenance equipment, since the entrance was only about three feet tall and four feet wide. One afternoon, on garbage day — which meant I had to wade through the garbage bags thrown out the windows of the apartments above mine into the alley — I saw my other "neighbor" move, then crawl out of, the grate blocking off the crawlspace and begin looking through the bags. He was an older, extremely pale white guy in a very stained orange dress shirt and powder-blue pants, who introduced himself as Mr. T and said it was nice to have a new neighbor because the "Reverend" wasn't great company.

My apartment was a tiny, approximately 5'x12' room which featured mice, no A/C, no oven, and a bathroom so small that when you sat on the toilet you had to have your knees sticking out of the doorway into the "living room." All this for a mere $750 a month in 1998 — what a bargain! But "at least I was in a safe area," my mom kept saying. Well, it seemed safe until my fourth night there when, as I lay awake in my coffin-sized bed wondering what in my life had led to the incredibly poor decision to move here, a pasty hand with a large pinky ring reached through my window, knocking the screen to the floor, and felt around in the air, tapping the thin wall of the apartment for a minute or so before slowly retreating back into the dark oblivion of my alleyway, not having found whatever it was it was looking for — "probably my neck" — I thought. I sat bolt-upright and awake for the next two nights.

Back in Manaus, I wasn't quite ready to sleep yet, so I decided I'd walk a little because it was too late to call Anna. The hotel was massive. The hallways were at least double the width of any other hotel hallways I'd ever seen, the ceilings were high, and there were huge ornate fans everywhere — it was just a beautiful place. I followed a few geckos out an open door to the patio and was surprised to look up and see a monster-sized river turtle looking at me, unperturbed. There were dozens of them hanging out near some pools and fountains, which were turned off for the night. They didn't seem to mind me as I approached them. I made a mental note to come down in the morning and get some pictures of them. The only wildlife I was accustomed to seeing at most of our hotels were ants, bedbugs, rats, and mosquitos.

I made another mental note to thank Sol for somehow getting approval to book this place. I was feeling a little tired and decided to leave my reptilian friends for the night and trek to my room. I was once again shocked to find a king-size bed with very clean sheets, featherbed, and the greatest mattress I had ever laid on, a working air conditioner (which was immediately turned to full blast), a waterfall shower, fluffy towels, and a large TV. I took a relaxing hot shower, suffered no electric shocks, and was pleased to find the room comfortably cool by the time I got out. I turned on the TV as I started unzipping my backpack and ended up watching *Jurassic Park* in Portuguese — because you always watch *Jurassic Park* when you flip to it on TV, whatever language it's in. The commercials featured bikini models in the Brazilian colors of green and yellow for whatever product was being sold — beer, cars, life insurance, home security. The go-to seemed to be bikini models in thongs. As Sam Neill was explaining how the use of frog DNA in dino-resurrection gave the creatures the ability to change their sex (spoiler — sorry), I decided to go to sleep. The crew would be arriving the next day and I wanted to explore the hotel grounds a little before they got in and we started working. I set an alarm for 8 a.m. and laid down in my luxurious bed. I was asleep before the raptors learned how to use doorknobs.

I woke up feeling well rested, hungry, and excited to explore. I made my way down to the complimentary breakfast spread and found a feast before me. There was every variety of fruit imaginable, numerous egg dishes to choose from, homemade cheeses, an omelet station, a great number of meats, and delicious tapioca pancakes made to order. There was also a huge selection of fresh juices (I sampled all of them, then mixed them, and drank more) and the best coffee I've ever had at a hotel.

I filled my plate, devoured everything on it in five minutes flat, then went up for seconds. I forced myself to eat the second plate a little slower and I looked around at my fellow diners while I chewed. The large banquet room was a mix of ethnicities, but a large percentage of the crowd looked like Brazilian tourists. They were easy to spot, because they were all gorgeous. The men were all perfectly toned and lounged effortlessly in their chairs. They all seemed to have six-pack abs and their shirts were unbuttoned to display them. The women were equally perfect in appearances and just as at ease in their demeanor. Quite a few were wearing thongs and tiny bikini tops — this was breakfast time, remember. The couples in the packed dining area's admiration for each other went beyond your normal public displays of affection. They were just all over each other. In the line for food, there was playful pinching of each other's butts, giggling, etc. At the tables, couples were feeding each other with their hands and mouths, stopping in between bites to make out, and a number of these couples were sitting on each other's laps while eating at the table.

None of the other Brazilians seemed to even notice. The foreign tourists definitely noticed, however. I saw a few women shooting angry looks at their husbands when they gave what they must have thought were discreet glances at the young, lithe, couples but were in reality obvious cartoon wolflike checkouts. I saw teenagers stare in open-mouthed awe at the young men and women — the best vacation of their lives, no doubt. This was breakfast. I couldn't imagine what I'd find by the pool.

I was not disappointed. The pool looked like a Pitbull video. I think you get the idea, so I won't go into more detail — let's just say that the few kids who were there were going to have a lot of questions for Google when they got back home. I left the pool and continued my exploration of the grounds. I found the turtles again, snapped some pictures, petted a couple of them, and moved on to the zoo. The Hotel Tropical had a fully operational zoo. I was worried that it would be one of those crappy, depressing zoos where you leave feeling terrible for the poor creatures contained in it, but it wasn't at all. All the animals appeared to be very healthy and well cared for. The enclosures were expansive and well maintained, and the information posted all over it was scientifically accurate and interesting. All in all, it was better than most zoos in the US. The only concerning thing was the lack of supervision. If I'd wanted to, I could have walked over and put my arm into the jaguar enclosure. But who would want to? I kind of liked the very un-American "stupid is supposed to hurt" attitude. If you stick your arm in a jaguar enclosure, you deserve whatever happens. We shouldn't need safety barriers to prevent you from doing something that might obviously lead you to lose a limb.

I walked back to the main lobby and past the pool once again, and sat at the bar enjoying a Skol and a burger for lunch. I figured Anna would be awake by then and called her to fill her in on the adventure thus far. She didn't believe my stories about the cabbies or about the breakfast thongs — but she was impressed with the description of the place. "Not quite like the places you book for our shoots." She said. It was a massive understatement.

The crew arrived as I was eating and contemplating all that I'd seen. I filled them in on my adventures as we all thanked Sol over and over for somehow getting approval for that place. After the Tropical, we "camped" on a boat for about a week as we travelled down the Amazon. We passed yachts and super yachts that must have cost over 200 million dollars — but we also passed rusting, broken-down, blood-and-filth covered sleeper boats — and we weren't on one! The boats we were on were comfortable, clean, and safe, and the kind folks helping us were friendly and personable. Yes, we slept on hammocks under mosquito nets, but we fell asleep and woke up to the sounds of the Amazon rainforest all around us. We had fresh fish and fruit for almost every meal — caught and picked the same day we were eating it. Juice from fruits I'd never heard of regularly and amazing Coffee and caipirinhas whenever we asked. If anything, the boats were more luxurious than the hotel.

Possibly just to make sure were weren't going to think every future shoot would be like this, our last three nights were spent sleeping in a single room of an old abandoned classroom in the middle of the rainforest. It was on the edge of a tribal territory and was, at one time, part of a school complex. Our "bedroom" still had a blackboard and some posters that made me think it was intended for young kids — but now contained some rusted metal bunk-bed frames. Mattresses were produced from a different building, and we were shown the bathroom — which reminded me of a public bathroom at a rundown beach — concrete, showers and toilet stalls missing doors, etc. The water had been shut off for an undetermined amount of time, so, as James volunteered to shower first, he received most of the brown, foul-smelling liquid that first came out. Laughing, he rejoined us in the bedroom, rolling a cigarette and grabbing some stale bread, and Guarana then said: "Ah yeah, this feels more like it. TVs Pat Spain, you bring us to the nicest places".

Chapter 4

Mapinguari – Rainforest Superhero

In the beginning, all things lived under the Earth, and were part of the Earth. Like the cicada, life was gestating, preparing to be born; and like the cicada also, it burst forth into the air after many, many years underground. All of the living things that came from the Earth, are made of the Earth. This is why we can eat plants, fruits, nuts, fish, birds, and all other life – because we are all made of the same substance. It's also why jaguars, snakes, caiman, and scavengers can eat us. We are all made of the same substance – Earth. Except for the Mapinguari. The Mapinguari is made from red wood and was not from the Earth like all other life. It emerged separately and must always be separate. It is of the Forest, not of the Earth. It protects the forest and keeps it in balance. Neither we men nor any other animal can eat the Mapinguari, because it is not made of Earth, we cannot digest it. Because we cannot eat it, and no other animal can eat it, we cannot kill it, because it is wrong to kill an animal that you are not going to eat. It would also be wrong because the Mapinguari is the Forest, and protects the Forest. Because the Mapinguari is not of the Earth, like we are, and because we cannot eat or kill it, and because it protects the forest – we must leave it alone. If any one of us ever sees or even hears a Mapinguari, we must leave that area forever. We must move our family, or our entire village, and never go back to where we saw or heard the Mapinguari, because that land belongs to it, and everything in that land is under its protection.

The Karitiana creation myth and Mapinguari legend, told to me by the elder of the tribe. It has never been shared with the Western world before (shared here with permission).

Hello there, and thank you for making it this far with me. We've come to the "cryptid" – or mysterious animals that may or may not exist – chapter of the book. This is either a very weird turn in the funny travel book you've been enjoying, or you were VERY confused by the first few chapters of the cryptozoology book you purchased. I will not be citing my sources here (most of them are my own notes and memories anyway). Feel free to Google anything I mention and write angry emails and nasty tweets about how I got the square mileage of the Amazon river basin wrong. This is not a paper to be published in a scientific journal; it is a collection of true stories from my personal experiences and some of my opinions. When making *Beast Hunter* we needed to cite at least two credited (peer-reviewed or expert-opinion) sources for every fact I stated on camera. There was a fact checker at Nat Geo whose job was to pick apart every line said. Most networks do not require this, but it's one of the reasons I love Nat Geo so much, and why Nat Geo is among the most respected brands in the world. But our job of making films about animals that may or may not exist did become very difficult as a result. There were so many retakes in order to throw in a "perhaps" or a "some experts say" that we ended up doing a five-minute reel of me just repeating phrases implying ambiguity in different intonations which we could cut in during editing. Actually we loved the scrutiny, and I feel it made the series much better than your run-of-the-mill crypto show filled with statements like, "that's definitely a werewolf" when someone hears a barred owl; or an episode with more night-vision footage than a want-to-be-actor's "break-out" video (regardless of whether the proposed animal is nocturnal or not), and lots of loud noises and Blair Witch-style nausea-inducing camera movements followed by "what's *THAT?!?*"; or – in my opinion, the biggest crime in this field – faked news stories or actors playing scientists. That is bullshit, I say!

There were a few things in *Beast Hunter* that were cut by

our fact checker which I would still argue were true. We lost a whole segment when I caught a hagfish because I said, "They aren't closely related to anything else, and they really aren't even a fish by a strict definition." I *may* have slightly overstated how different they are evolutionarily, but I still maintain that what I said was true. My friend Zeb, a real marine biologist, is probably cringing reading this, but it's that kind of scrutiny and adherence to the truth that I think set our show apart. Anyway, there is no fact checker on this book, other than you, dear reader, so check away but, as I said, these are mostly my own thoughts, opinions, and experiences.

In case you haven't figured it out yet, I am a nerd. Not like, "I cannot wait for the new episodes of Mandalorian to be released!" – a real nerd; specifically, a science nerd. This differs from the so-hot-right-now comic-book/sci-fi nerd. Sure, I liked *Fringe* as much as the next guy, I've read all *A Song of Ice and Fire* books to date, and my high-school friends and I stayed in on Friday nights to watch *The X-Files*, but my true nerd status really becomes apparent whenever a conversation strays into any topic in biology. I advocated for the name "Darwin" if our first child was a boy, and when we found out we were having a daughter I tried to convince Anna it would still make a great middle name. We ended up naming her Luna after the amazingly beautiful and mysterious *Actias luna*, the luna moth. Yes, I'm aware that Luna Lovegood is a character in one of my favorite book series – she's one of Anna's and my favorite characters, in fact, but that's an added bonus for the name rather than a driving force. Our son is named Wallace Charles after Alfred Russel Wallace, Charles Darwin, and Charles Fort.

I was a teaching assistant for multiple chemistry and biology labs and audited extra biology and philosophy classes – for fun. I traveled to Maryland to observe horseshoe crabs mating – again, for fun. One of the only real fights I can remember getting into with my best friend since birth was when we were eight and he insisted that crabs were amphibians. The only TV shows I watched in the eighties and nineties were nature programs. Whenever I was sick and off school I was allowed to rent anything I wanted from the video store. My pick was always a volume of *Life on Earth*. David Attenborough, Alfred Russel Wallace, and Charles Darwin were my childhood heroes, and remain my adult heroes – in addition to Harry Marshall, the man responsible for sending me on all of these adventures and forever changing the course of my life. He also makes damn fine TV.

When I left home at 16 and lived on my own for the first time it was for a marine biology internship in Maine. A friend asked what the nightlife was like in southern Maine. I replied, with no hesitation or sense of irony, "Great! It's really awesome! There are foxes, raccoons, lightning bugs, polyphemus moths, and so far I've spotted two species of owls!" I also read the *Fortean Times* and *CryptoZooNews*, and most of the people I follow on social media are naturalists. Don't worry, though – I won't get *too* scientific in this chapter (and there will be poop jokes).

I say all of this because, in recent years, there has been a move towards hijacking nerd culture by moderately cool people. An actor who can't quite cut it turns to fantasy shows and suddenly he's a heartthrob. A few years back, even Charlie Sheen "led a search for the Loch Ness Monster." I happened to be in Scotland, investigating the same monster at the same time he was, and heard some horror stories from the locals about his behavior in their beautiful country. I am not a person who does this stuff for the attention – I do it because I love it and am fascinated by it, and because I think it doesn't do science any favors to simply write off the things that sound bizarre.

Too many scientists forget that the general public does not consist primarily of other scientists, and most people would rather hear about the *possibility* of a bipedal intelligent ape walking through the Great North Woods than the reality of the new barnacle you discovered. Run with that, talk about the *possibility*. It will get people listening. Then throw in some stuff about wolverines, the re-introduction of wolves, and pine martens, and make them things that people, real people, will find interesting. Throw in some jokes, give some sexy facts – more people would have been interested in your lame barnacle if you led with it having the largest penis to body ratio of any animal in the world. It's over six times the total length of its body! That's CRAZY! And fascinating! And memorable. Where do they keep it? How do ... I'm getting sidetracked; the point is — don't refuse to talk about something because you think it sounds silly. Getting people outside for a homemade Bigfoot expedition still gets them outside, and they *will* see other amazing and exciting things even if they don't see a Sasquatch. A generation of Bigfoot hunters might turn into conservationists, or field biologists, or maybe lawyers who will want to protect the land they loved exploring as a kid. Another interesting side effect of not immediately writing these things off, all of you close-minded scientists out there, is that sometimes, *sometimes*, you might find that there is actually *something* to these stories. If you go out there, use your scientific training, open your mind, dispel disbelief and really look at the facts and evidence, you might surprise yourself, like I did with the Mapinguari and others.

I am an open-minded skeptic at heart, and I approached everything around *Beast Hunter* as such. There is a famous quote regarding Occam's razor that goes something like: "When you hear hoof beats in the distance, you don't think it's a herd of unicorns. You think of horses, and you're probably correct." I also think of horses, but am willing to be shown the evidence of unicorns. On the show, I did have a "mistaken identity" theory for each cryptid in the series; however, I was more interested in the cultural significance of each myth than its veracity.

Like most things in cryptozoology, the Mapinguari seems, at

least on the surface, batshit crazy. It's supposedly a 15–20' tall, one-eyed monster with a mouth in the middle of its chest that kills anyone abusing the forest, and smells so bad that you will certainly pass out, and possibly die, from one whiff of its BO. It also has all of the other important accoutrements of a good nasty beastie – fangs dripping with venom, medusa-like "kill you with a glance" eye, long and sharp claws, and a scream that can stop your heart. Oh, and an ornithologist thinks it's a living species of an animal which most scientists believe went extinct about 8000 years ago. However, also like many things in cryptozoology, if you push past the first instinct to mockingly dismiss it out of hand, a bizarre but entirely believable narrative starts to unfurl.

We spent a fair amount of time with two tribes of indigenous people, the Sateré-Mawé and Karitiana, discussing their beliefs about the Mapinguari – their "truths" for this creature. We stopped in on another half-dozen or so other tribal groups along the river and asked them the same general questions. We also visited fish and produce markets all over Amazonia and Rondonia and asked random urban dwellers in the markets the same questions. Ninety-nine percent of these "interviews" never made it into the episode – less than half were probably even filmed – but they gave us a sense of what people believed to be true, and where the discrepancies were in those beliefs. They provided context for the episode and a basis for this chapter.

When you sort through the vastly divergent tales of this creature from all over the Brazilian Amazon you start to realize that the people, generally indigenous tribes, living in the regions where this animal has been spotted describe a very different beast than their neighbors in the city. You also realize that the tribes in the remote rainforest don't talk about any of the bizarre characteristics that their urban brethren are so fond of. A height of 15–20' tall becomes 6–8'; the "one eye" becomes a "large nose" or "pinched look"; the mouth in its chest filled with venom-tipped fangs becomes an odd coloration, and either mucous or some other slimy secretion near its chest and back; the smell "so strong it can make you pass out or even kill you" becomes a very strong, foul odor that can make you nauseous – okay, the city folk may have gotten that one pretty close. Most importantly – and something I learned first-hand from the tribes, whom I believe hadn't shared this with any Westerner before me – the "kill you with a glance" look and "deadly cry" become, not deadly, but so life-changing that death would only be one short step away.

Catching a fleeting glimpse or hearing the mournful call are not "said to" but will absolutely bring about a major change in your life. This creature, this Mapinguari, is so feared, not because seeing or hearing one will kill you, but because after the encounter you, your family, and your entire tribe must never return to its location. Out of respect for this demi-god, you must leave it alone, because this animal is "other" – it is not "made of the same stuff as people." Although it is a living, breathing, flesh-and-blood creature, it is the embodiment of the forest itself.

Right from the beginning, this distinction – myth versus real creature – seemed to be the key to presenting the story of the Mapinguari – this "urban legend" in the truest sense of the word, and the believable, if outlandish, reality behind it. There is a belief among certain groups that the Mapinguari doesn't live on the same level of existence as we do. They would say, "It's real, but you can only see it if you do drugs with the tribes," or, "If you do something to open your eyes to the forest." This seems on the surface like a mark against it being a real creature, but actually goes a long way towards explaining some of its more bizarre traits. It makes sense in a weird way – myth or reality, the Mapinguari is special. To see it, to understand it, you yourself have to change; you have to change not only who you are, but how you see the world. You have to open yourself to all possibilities. This personal transformation is critical to unlocking any secrets about this creature.

Ben, our brilliant and mad episode producer, suggested I take ayahuasca and describe the things I saw. Harry disagreed. Not because he was against my taking psychotropic drugs – in fact, he thought it sounded like a good plan on our downtime – but, as he said, "It's been done, I've seen it, I don't need to see it again. And besides, if Pat is out of his mind for another few days, we'll be way off schedule." I had already fought to do the Tucandeira ceremony, to show the tribes that they could trust me, and Ben had an inkling that this would be my transformative event. We started talking through it in the context of change – changing me, my perceptions, my notions of "real."

Ben determined that the episode and all revelations within it would be presented through the new perspective I would have gained after the ceremony. As we talked it through, we decided that only something so outrageous, so contrary to anything that seems like a good idea, something that makes so little sense on a cerebral level, could truly open my eyes to the "hidden world" of the forest. None of us could have known then just how correct he was. The Tucandeira was the key to my understanding the Mapinguari, though not in the way we expected.

After the ceremony, I had to admit I most certainly did *not* see the Mapinguari while hallucinating from the pain. My visions were all ant related. They were terrible, but they didn't contain any one-eyed beast trying to eat me, thankfully. Ben was a bit disappointed, but he knew a literal vision of the creature was a long shot. That's not to say I wasn't changed by the experience, though. The main reason I participated in the ceremony was to "open my eyes to the forest," and show the tribe I respected them and was deserving of hearing the truth behind the stories that only they had access to – a way to gain that hidden knowledge. Not figuratively, not "I see the forest differently now," but literally. I would not be brazen enough to say I was "a member of the tribe" – I don't think I could ever earn that right. That means being a daily part of a community that supports and protects each other. Without moving there, or growing up there, or truly "being" there, I wouldn't feel like I'd earned the honor of calling myself that, but I had shown them respect, and the Pateré-Mawé, Karitiana, and others honored respect. They deemed me worthy of hearing their ancient stories and traditions, allowing me to see the forest as they do – to see "the hidden world." It *was* an honor, and remains so.

People in the cities have it wrong, like a bad translation. For an outsider to "know" the Mapinguari, they have to no longer be an outsider – they must become one of the people who live in the Mapinguari's forest. This can be through various rituals, some of which involve hallucinogens, others bullet ants, all changing who you are and how you see things. These rituals are always a part of you, as any experience is – they make you think about everything in your life differently because you are newly equipped to do so. It's like waking up with a third arm – you are different after it, and your world is forever changed. Also, the Mapinguari is not a spirit animal – it is a real creature, but when the tribe says "you can't see it" they don't mean it's impossible, they mean it two ways – "YOU can't see it," meaning "only WE can see it," and "You *CAN'T* see it," as in "You shouldn't" – "If you do, you have to move your entire village away from the spot and never go back."

I believe that it was because of my participation in the bullet-ant ritual that the Karitiana tribe felt they could trust me enough to share the legend that started this chapter, and know it is the reason the Pateré-Mawé shared their stories and views with me. They both told me I was the first person from outside the tribe they had shared these with. I have shared the creation story here, with their permission, because I believe it is critical in explaining how a very smart and humble ornithologist (Dr. Oren) and a reasonably sane, reasonably intelligent biologist (me) can say they believe there is a strong possibility that an animal most people think has been extinct for thousands of years is still wandering around the Amazon.

With that hopefully intriguing intro, I present the myth and reality of the Mapinguari, as told in small villages and large cities throughout Brazil.

Descriptors of the mythical Mapinguari:

- One eye
- Covered in hair
- Mouth in chest
- Fangs that drip with venom
- Huge sharp claws
- A smell so bad it can kill you
- Eyes that either hypnotize or kill if you look into them
- A cry that can knock you out or kill you
- Huge, up to 20' tall
- Walks on two legs
- Huge claws
- Feet are backwards so the tracks will lead potential poachers in the wrong direction (this trait is also associated with other mythical creatures like the Kuripira)
- Very aggressive, protects forest from poachers/over-harvesting
- Lives anywhere it's needed – where the forest is being exploited or kids are misbehaving
- Seen only by people who have had "their eyes open to the forest" through various rituals, generally involving hallucinogens. The Mapinguari is only real to those initiates; it lives on a higher plain of existence, like a demi-god

Sounds like your typical boogeyman with an oddly liberal twist, right? "You'd better eat your organic, fair-trade, acai berries, Paxton, or the Mapinguari will be very sad. He doesn't want anything from his forest to be wasted, and you've barely touched your super-grains!" Besides kids destined to be dangerously overconfident, he also targets poachers and anyone practicing unsustainable farming techniques. Sort of a 20' tall Leng Ouch with venomous fangs.

I like this Mapinguari. The Massachusetts liberal in me likes this "balancing of the scales," this Iron Man-like righting of eco-wrongs by a lone individual. This Mapinguari can mimic the footprints of other animals and lead you to your doom in the middle of the forest if you are hunting endangered species or pregnant animals. It will destroy your logging equipment if you are practicing unsustainable harvesting techniques, or cutting down ancient, sacred, trees. It protects and preserves the native population's rights to their own land. It is also, unfortunately, very clearly a legend.

The other Mapinguari, the "real creature," is the one talked about in small villages and isolated tribes deep in the Amazonian rainforest. The animal that these tribes describe and call the Mapinguari is described thusly:

- 6–8' tall
- covered in fur
- small eyes
- large nose
- mouth-like marking on its chest or back, with a thick, stinky excretion
- four large canine teeth
- huge claws
- walks on all fours, and rears up on two when threatened
- some say aggressive, some say not
- vegetarian, but will defend itself violently and kill people or animals if it's threatened

- very strong foul odor
- backwards facing feet
- loud, low, mournful cry
- very thick, nearly impenetrable skin except on the face and part of the belly (it requires an extra-large bullet to even hurt one)
- crepuscular, but seen during the day, and occasionally at night
- lives in very remote Amazon basin, in thick forest

The two animals share some characteristics, and it's easy to see where the myth came from when you have all of the "facts" in front of you. Looking at this second description, a couple of animals come to mind – one is well known and loved by kids around the world thanks to numerous cartoon depictions of its bizarre nose, and another has been extinct for over 8000 years.

I believe that many sightings can be explained by the well-known if somewhat misunderstood and reclusive giant anteater. This truly bizarre creature is a lumbering contradiction. Seeing one up close, it's hard to decide if you want to laugh, scream, hug it, or run away in terror. It has a drunken appearance to its gait; its snout is stretched to Pinocchio proportions; it has fierce looking claws on muscular arms and an over-the-top frilly tail; it emits a potent stench all of the time, but when threatened the smell takes on hormonal properties and can be overwhelming; the noises it produces seem alien and obscene; and it is known to stand on its hind legs, making it almost six feet tall, and thrash out at a potential assailant with its five-inch claws. Anyone coming upon one of these guys unexpectedly can be forgiven for assuming they just survived an attack by a mythical monster.

Some of the other sightings I believe are due to a close relative of the anteater, the aforementioned, supposed-to-be-extinct-in-the-Pliocene beast. I am referring, of course, to megatherium – the giant ground sloth. This seems like a huge leap for a (debatably) respectable, (debatably) rational, and (by some measures) sane biologist to make, but hear me out. I believe I can convince most skeptics that it's at least possible that this species survived much, much later than the scientific community accepts.

Muddying the waters are the powers of oral tradition among the indigenous tribes in the regions. A researcher I met with told me about a particular tribe in Chile who hadn't been to their native lands in two generations due to political upheaval, but the stories and legends from those lands are instilled in each new member. He was able to accompany them when they finally returned and was amazed to see young people who had never personally encountered the flora and fauna of the region immediately recognize it, and even explain their lifecycle, diet, hunting grounds, etc., based on the stories from the elders they had grown up with. Could some of the reports of ground-sloth sightings feel so authentic because the sighters' relatives truly did see and even hunt ground sloths thousands of years ago, but the stories have remained fresh thanks to oral traditions? Generational time is hard to measure, but let's take an average lifespan of 70 for an individual in the tribe in question. Let's also say that, by 5 years old, lifelong memories can be formed. A man in this tribe born in 1800 will live until 1870 – let's say that his grandson, or great-grandson, will be born in 1860 – meaning that by the time *he* dies (1930) he will have heard first-hand accounts of events from 1805, and his kin, born in 1925, will in 1995 be able to recall events from 1805 that he heard only second hand. In this way, 8000 years isn't really *that* distant.

Sightings of the giant ground sloth have been reported since European explorers first trekked through South America, though one can draw their own conclusion as to their veracity. Reports of hulking, unwieldy beasts reached mass audiences when such respected scientists and writers such as Ray Lancaster and my family's own Charles Fort spoke and wrote about them in the late nineteenth and early twentieth centuries, both stating that they believed this creature was still living in the dense jungles and mountaintops of South America. These sightings have never stopped, but sightings are far from proof. Where the megatherium differs from many other cryptids is that we know that it is real. We have many full skeletons, and even a fair amount of skin and fur from these creatures. My favorite skeleton, and the one I've spent the most time with, is in the Harvard Museum of Comparative Zoology. It was discovered in a tar pit in beautiful New Jersey. (Despite popular opinion, the entire state of NJ is not one massive tar pit, but there are a few famous ones there.)

I spent many hours in college at the HMCZ, and much of that time was spent marveling at the magnificent forms of their ground-sloth skeleton, stuffed thylacine, and a pickled coelacanth. The coelacanth is sort of the unofficial symbol of cryptozoology – it even appears on the official logo of the International Cryptozoology Museum. Bigfoot might get all of the attention from the masses, but everyone in cryptozoology loves that bony-finned bastard. It gives us all hope. The fish is what science calls a "Lazarus species," meaning a species whose extinction was accepted as scientific fact, until a live one showed up. This happens a lot more frequently than you'd expect. In fact, about 30% of all mammals declared extinct in the last few centuries have turned up alive. And it's not just mammals that science has pulled a "Madeline Usher" on – my friend's sister, Emily Fountain, made a name for herself by documenting living species of weevils declared extinct in New Zealand. Various insect, fish, amphibian, reptile, bird, and plant species pop up in the news every year when they are rediscovered, especially if the story is particularly bizarre like a venomous mammal in Cuba (the Cuban Solenodon), 30 "land lobsters" or "walking sausages" discovered under a single shrub (the Lord Howe

Island Stick Insect), or a whale (the pygmy right whale). So why, you may ask, is the coelacanth so special?

There are a few things that make an animal sexy in public opinion, and thus worthy of attention. There needs to be a feature about it that stands out and makes it stick in your head, since it's competing with the names of who the various Kardashians are dating and the lyrics to "Ice Ice Baby" for brain space. They can be very cute, like baby seals, very dangerous, like black mambas (it helps to have an Uma Thurman character named after said dangerous animal), or just plain impressive like a lion or whale. Sometimes, a random fact about the creature is enough to help embed it in our collective consciousness – binturongs smell like popcorn, an anteater's tongue is two feet long, and bonobos use sex to resolve conflicts. Lastly, in our always-online culture, a well-made meme ensures everyone talks about the animal featured, at least for a short time. Goats screaming Taylor Swift songs, a kid sleeping on a giant snake "like a boss," and every video Ze Frank has made immediately come to mind. Oh and cats. So. Many. Cats.

The coelacanth enjoyed some time in the pop-culture zeitgeist thanks to all of the above, except it's not "super cute." It's pretty big, has gnarly teeth, and has a face that's sufficiently awkward enough for memes. Primarily, though, it's notable for its length of absence from our "living species" lexicon – 65 million years, give or take. When it showed up again in a South African fish market in 1938 it made quite a stir. Cryptozoology loves it because not only is it an extreme Lazarus species, but also a fantastic example of a species known by indigenous people but written off by mainstream scientists as myth. The locals had been eating it for years and could even describe its habitat, but science didn't pay attention until it was seen by a white dude. There are many examples of this – native stories just taken as myths by the wide world until a Western scientist gives the animal a Latin name. Among the most famous are the okapi, platypus, and the mountain gorilla, but less well known and recent are the ulama, or Sri Lankan Devil Bird – a bird with devil-like horns whose blood-curdling scream was said to be an omen of death. In 2001, science (which had poo-pooed this creature as local folklore for centuries) found a new, large, species of horned owl, the spot-bellied eagle owl, whose appearance and cry perfectly matched the devil bird. There was also the bondegezous, a creature believed by locals to be the embodiment of their ancestors' spirits in a Western Indonesian culture. It wasn't until 1995 that a newly "discovered" marsupial, the dingiso, was officially accepted as a real creature.

The thylacine (Tasmanian tiger) also enjoys a special place in the annals of cryptozoology. Many people believe that it illustrates that "extinct" is a process rather than a final pronouncement – much like how many doctors are now looking at death. There is "locally extinct," which means the animal is no longer found in an area where it was once prominent, like the buffalo in much of the US; "extinct in the wild" which means the animal is no longer found in the wild, but there is a strong population in zoos and other sanctuaries, like the axolotl; "functionally extinct" which means there may still be some individuals in the wild, but not enough to play a significant role in the ecosystem or maintain a genetically diverse breeding population – in fact, there might only be a few aging individuals, like the baiji dolphin; there is then the classic "extinct," meaning no individuals remain alive. This has a finality that many conservative biologists are hesitant to declare with modern species, instead opting for "functionally extinct" in many cases. Many animals classified as "extinct in the wild" are really "functionally extinct in the wild."

Depending on who you talk to, the thylacine is either functionally extinct or simply extinct. It's believed that the last one died in Hobart Zoo in 1936. It's the subject of a short film reel from 1933, and a few other clips from the same period –

the only scientifically accepted footage of a living thylacine. Sightings have been reported consistently in Australia and Tasmania since their alleged "extinction," often by well-respected, highly trained individuals such as park rangers. Scat, hair, and footprints have also been recovered in recent years, leading many scientists to conclude that this creature may not deserve the finality of being declared extinct. It also manages to garner some degree of scientific acceptance for its continued existence, despite the vast majority of evidence pointing in the other direction. This begs the question – why the thylacine and no other cryptid?

Not to get too off-topic, but the crypto-community shows even more love for the thylacine than the coelacanth as the unofficial mascot of de-extinction. Numerous projects have been put forward to use genetic material from preserved specimens to produce a living thylacine. This is theoretically possible, and an extinct Pyrenean ibex was born to a surrogate goat in 2003, but only lived for seven minutes. It is believed that we have the potential to resurrect species like the wooly mammoth, the passenger pigeon, the thylacine, and perhaps the giant ground sloth.

The ground sloth takes the same concepts presented by the two species above – the coelacanth and the thylacine – and pushes them just over the fuzzy line of "scientifically acceptable possibility" into the realm of "barely tolerated eccentric weirdo" – which is one step below "flat-earth asshole." It went extinct *just* a bit too long ago, it's big enough that anyone might think, "We surely would have seen something *that* large!" and the people sighting it are not Westerners but generally indigenous peoples, whose sightings the West tends to believe count for less than our own. (This is a hard truth that the scientific community MUST own up to, and actively work to correct.) Leaving aside this last point, I can understand people thinking the previous two – those who haven't been to the Amazon, that is.

So, my budding biologist-self spent a fair amount of time

over four years studying the remains of three of the superstars of cryptozoology. It's hard to not want to see a live one when you've spent so much time thinking about what they must have been like. Even so, I was not optimistic of a chance encounter with a ground sloth when I stepped off the plane in Manaus. My thinking was more in line with accepted scientific "fact." And the Man says:

- Ground sloths went extinct on mainland North and South America about 8–10 thousand years ago
- Some ground sloths in the Caribbean lasted about another 5–6 thousand years, until people showed up
- In both locations, they were either hunted to extinction by humans or somehow killed off due to habitat destruction or losing their resources/food sources
- They had an osteoderm – a very thick bony skin covering – all over their body, aside from the stomach and face
- They were primarily vegetarian, but probably aggressive if threatened
- They likely moved on four legs, but reared up onto two as a defensive posture or to reach vegetation that was high up
- The largest (megatherium) would have been a bit larger than a modern elephant at almost 9000 pounds and 20 feet long, though most were significantly smaller, in the 7–12 foot range
- Their huge claws could not be retracted and the way they carried them caused their tracks to appear distorted, and facing backwards
- They were covered in thick fur of varying colors
- They had small eyes
- The had a large, broad nose
- Their teeth were like those of modern sloths with 4 large canines

- They had massive claws
- They were likely diurnal
- They had a broad range all over North and South America

And what we are less sure of, but can make a logical inference on, based on living sloths:

- There was a V-shaped, dark marking on its chest or back with a thick, stinky, excretion
- They had a very strong foul odor
- They had a loud cry

Are these traits sounding familiar? Yeah, you're not the only one who thinks so. Renowned ornithologist Dr. David Oren heard the legends of the Mapinguari the 1980s and pieced the puzzle together. He made a stir in the mid-nineties when he published his findings, which were compelling. Unsurprisingly, the scientific community acted swiftly to disavow him and his research.

Dr. Oren is hesitant to speak about the Mapinguari these days – maybe it's the decades of failed expeditions to find definitive proof of one, maybe it's the isolation he's been subjected to in the remote Amazon, or maybe it's the ridicule he suffered after trying to get scientists to admit that we just might not know everything – likely it's a combination of all of the above. It's clear that unlike Dr. Jeff Meldrum (the Bigfoot guy), Dr. Oren has no interest in being the "giant sloth" guy. I was lucky enough to meet with him in a remote town on the outskirts of the state of Rondonia, Brazil. The town used to be the start of a vast rail-shipping network, but the trains have sat idle and rusting for decades. We met in the abandoned central station, in an old-fashioned train car once used as a mobile classroom. We found it in an advanced state of decay, littered with used condoms, old cushions, mouse shit, and graffiti. Dr. Oren and

I sat in bench seats designed for children and chuckled at the oddness of our surroundings. "Ah, the majesty of television production," he said, as Ben flicked away a decade of detritus to find a handhold and frame the shot. I found David incredibly engaging, intelligent, and passionate.

In many ways, he's a stereotype of an ex-pat field biologist. He has a friendly round face, smiles a bit ruefully when he talks about his years in the field, sports a full bushy mustache, and has pale blue eyes that light up when he speaks about his true passion of birds. When we met, he wore jeans and a nondescript button-down shirt, the adopted uniform of most non-lab biologists. He isn't interested in cryptozoology and mythology – he's interested in biology. He has a collection of footprints, hair, and scat from unknown animals associated with the Mapinguari which he "needs to get tested one day soon." He can also replicate practically any animal call he's ever heard and regularly whistles bird calls that are accurate enough to fool the locals. He allowed us to record him making a Mapinguari call, which immediately reminded me of a sloth call I'd recorded in Costa Rica years before, but deeper, as if made by larger vocal chords. He said no other animal in Brazil sounded like that.

Dr. Oren had come to believe the Mapinguari was a ground sloth after hearing a description of the creature from a "well-respected contact," and mentally comparing the descriptions to all-known animals – the ground sloth comes out the winner. He went in search of it for himself after personally hearing the call and when a local guide told him it was the Mapinguari. To Dr. Oren it sounded like a lower, longer, sloth call. When asked how it could have survived, he used the powerful argument of vast swaths of the Amazon being unexplored (as much as 95% according to some reports), abundant resources for the creatures, small numbers required for a breeding population of a large, long-lived, mammal, and the difficulties of getting to the regions where it is "known" to live. If you combine this with the creation story from the start of this chapter, and the fact that ground sloths were killed off by people, I believe you have a scenario for a remnant population.

Put it this way – we have an animal who in unlikely to have had a large home range. Looking at modern sloths, some of whom spend their entire lives in one tree, they would likely not have covered much ground except for when searching for a mate. We have a region of Brazil only inhabited by either uncontacted native tribes (tribes with no contact whatsoever with the Western world), or tribes with very limited, governmentally controlled outside contact (such as the ones I met after a thorough health screening and receiving special permission from the Brazilian government). These tribes have not only never hunted the Mapinguari but actually set aside nature preserves for them by clearing out of any areas where one is seen or heard. This practice has been going on for as long as the tribe has been in existence. This gives skeptics a scenario where it is in fact not just possible but likely that a small population of the animals survived, unharassed by the outside world and all humans, well beyond the time that the rest of their species died out – maybe even into present day – as the rest of them died out as a direct result of human activity.

Speaking with Dr. Oren was exciting, but I was still unconvinced. I hadn't met with the Karitiana yet, and their story was the final piece in the puzzle for me. Dr. Oren told us about an area where he had collected footprints (one of which he showed us), hair samples, and droppings that he believed were from a ground sloth. He said that most natives wouldn't go into the forest there, but would lead us to the edges. David, like most people, thought the natives feared the call of the Mapinguari because they believe seeing or hearing it would kill them, but as I stated above, this is an inaccurate depiction of the reality – it's a story for the uninitiated. They don't believe that seeing or hearing it would "kill" them, but do believe that the impacts of seeing or hearing one would be as profound, meaning they would have to leave an area and never return, so they actively avoid the possibility. Even so, the other version still gets the point across – "we aren't going to take you there" – and accomplishes the task of keeping people out of that region of the forest. Dr. Oren told us about the Karitiana, a tribe who might lead us to the edges, shook our hands, and left the abandoned railyard.

We packed up, boarded yet another plane, and went to the region he had described. We found The Karitiana, a tribe of less than 300 individuals with virtually no contact with the outside world, and convinced a young man to lead us. They reiterated what Dr. Oren had told us: "We won't go there, and you shouldn't either." Luckily, I was still visibly blue from my bullet-ant ritual. They asked about this and all shook hands with me after hearing about the ordeal. Although they were not Sateré-Mawé, they knew of the ritual and immediately accepted me and treated me as they would a visiting Sateré-Mawé. This is why they told me their creation myth after I asked about the Mapinguari, and why they agreed to bring us to the region where one had been spotted years before. However, they still would not go with us into the interior of that forest.

One of them, a man named Giovaldio, told us in confidence that he had seen and even shot at a Mapinguari a couple of years before. His friends teased him and said he'd been scared of a wild pig, but he insisted it was a Mapinguari. When I started showing him pictures of various animals on an iPad he identified all of the ones he could (most Brazilian animals), admitted to the ones he couldn't without guessing (African, Asian, and other wildlife), making references to a few but admitting he didn't know (such as a tiger – "that looks a little like a big jaguar, but it's an animal I've never seen"), and everything led me to believe he was telling the complete truth. When I showed him a giant ground sloth re-creation from a museum, he became very excited, saying, "Wow! That looks like a Mapinguari! Where did you get this picture? Can I look at it more closely?" I handed over the iPad and he started saying, more to himself than to us, "Its claws and hands looked like that, it didn't stand quite this way, it looked a bit bigger towards the bottom. I think its eyes were a little smaller and its fur was definitely a different color, but yes, yes, this is it." Then to us, "Yes! This is a Mapinguari! Where did you get this picture? Can I show my friends? I've been trying to describe it for years, but you have a picture of it! Can I show them?" Of course he could, we said. He anxiously called them over and started going through the description again, triumphant.

I genuinely believed him. There was no hint of faking it and no reason to do so. He seemed genuinely ashamed that he had shot at a Mapinguari – he said it was purely self-preservation, but he still felt terrible about it. He wasn't the reason we were there, there was no promise of people to follow after us if he had a good story – in fact, we had come across him accidentally, so he wasn't prepped to tell us "what we wanted to hear." His story seemed completely real, and the emotion and excitement would have been very hard to fake. It was hard to admit, but I believed that this man had seen a giant ground sloth two years before we met him.

His description of his encounter is well documented in the episode of *Beast Hunter*, and I won't rehash it here other than to say the part of the Mapinguari's hand in the filmed reenactment of that story involved a rubber werewolf glove that was worn alternately by each member of the crew and numerous members of the tribe. The glove also made appearances at various airports, hotels, and while paying for goods from surprised local vendors.

After hearing Givaldio's story, I was even more excited to get out into the field to find one myself, especially with my new belief that there was actually something to find besides a great story. There was the chance that I could actually document a living ground sloth! Once again, our excursion that night is well documented in the episode of the TV show, and I promised at the opening of this book not to go over what you have already seen or can see easily by snagging a copy of the show (shameless self-promotion). What I will add, though, is that James and I were not faking or playing this up at all. We genuinely did hear a call that was exactly what Dr. Oren described. We heard it 4–5 times, moving away from us. When we got back to the truck, Giovaldio and the other men had heard it as well and were a bit freaked out, saying we really needed to leave this place. They confirmed that no known animal made this noise, but did not agree that it was a Mapinguari, still not fully trusting us despite my cred as an honorary Sateré-Mawé (which was likely the only reason they'd agreed to bring us to that area in the first place) – they just said we all needed to leave and not come back, ever.

So, to sum it up and officially go on the record, I do now believe that the Mapinguari is likely a giant ground sloth and that there is a remnant population in the Amazon rainforest. I believe this because:

- The descriptions of the mapinguari match up with descriptions of ground sloths
- We know ground sloths lived in this region at some point
  - Ground sloths were hunted to extinction or their habitats were destroyed everywhere else by humans
  - The tribes in the region where the Mapinguari is believed to exist revere and fear it so much that they leave any area where one is seen or heard and never return, thereby creating nature preserves for these creatures. The Brazilian government's protection of tribal lands also protects the land from those not in the tribe.
- The eyewitnesses are credible and believable

- I heard a call myself that perfectly fit the descriptions, cannot be identified as anything else, and sounded exactly like a low-pitched sloth call

What came back to me as I was leaving Brazil is Dr. Oren's last words to us. As I turned to walk away, like a scene out of a movie, David said: "I really do believe it's there, you know."

I nodded "Yeah, I can see that," and smiled.

David went on: "You don't – think it's there I mean. That's okay, don't worry about it," he said as I started to apologize and explain that I just wasn't sure at that time. "It's not a bad thing. But watch out – once you do believe, it's really hard to walk away from." And he gave a sad hangdog smile.

That smile has stuck with me all these years. After hearing from our guides that we needed to leave I immediately wanted to go back. Even now I want very badly to go back to that spot in the forest and sit there for days and nights trying to hear the call again, to get footage of the creature making it and show the world there is still a monster out there in the deepest forest of Brazil, crying into the night.

Chapter Five

"Herpes Bees"

While filming *Beast Hunter* I was lucky enough to hear some fantastic first-hand accounts of mysterious and possibly unknown animals. Many of these, or at least one, I hope you'll agree by this point in the book, seem scientifically plausible. While these stories are astounding – the potential for large undiscovered creatures in the modern era – and exciting, some of my favorite stories were the clearly absurd and impossible ones. The ones where the creature in question breaks all known laws of biology and physics; where it talks to people, maybe telepathically; where it flits in and out of existence, or it morphs at will into a completely different genus. Many people write these off immediately, even get embarrassed hearing them, but not me. I love that shit. I try to cut through the insane-sounding surface and get to a possible grain of truth, or just determine that it's a great work of fiction. Either way, these stories are always fun.

In some cases, like the Mongolian Death Worm, you can find a cohesive underlying story that makes logical sense, reasons and explanations behind the outrageous tales. In other instances, like a man who told me a dinosaur almost killed him, there is clearly nothing but a good campfire story there. When these extremely tall-tales – which can range from the whimsical, the surreal, and the grotesque – venture into the category of "so terrible it's laughable," they are known collectively as "Herpes bees" by our crew, a term coined during our time in Brazil.

There is a rich story-telling tradition throughout the Amazon, and the legends, as outrageous as they seem, all serve a purpose for the local communities and tribes. Some of the cadre of characters that appear in these stories are:

Curupira, an elfin creature with red hair and backwards feet. This helpful little demon protects the forest. You're safe from his tricks as long as you respect the natural balance of things. If you take more than you need, hunt an animal that is caring for its young, or disrespect the forest in any way, he will lead you deep into the heart of the jungle and get you hopelessly lost, produce illusionary images that will drive you mad, or torment you with creepy sounds until you lose your mind. Bottom line – don't mess with the Amazon rainforest. There's the Cuca and Homem de Saco ("Sack Man"), both stories are used to scare kids into behaving. Sack Man is literally a dude who drags kids away in a sack. That is some messed up "scared straight" stuff right there. There's the lobisomeme – the Brazilian version of a werewolf which serves as a parable about following the laws. Iara lures men to live with her underwater. When people disappear in the jungle, it gives the family some peace to know they are not dead, but are instead happy with Iara, and they could not have resisted her call even if they wanted to. Encantado is someone who is magically trapped in another dimension, living an eternal but unfruitful life (usually a punishment for pursuing riches at any cost, or doing some major wrong).

One of my favorites is the Boto, also sometimes called Encantado, to make this extra confusing. The Boto is a pink river dolphin who occasionally turns most of his body into a handsome man, sometimes young and strong, sometimes old and with a bald spot, who women are "inexplicably drawn to," but he always retains some of his dolphin parts. Namely, his blowhole and an abnormally large penis. He wears a suit to hide his penis (regrettably, we all do) and a hat to hide the blowhole. Sometimes, he's only a man from the waist up (mermaid style), and other times he has legs, but there is always a blowhole on his head and the old Dirk Diggler below the belt. When in human or half-human form this creature likes nothing more than to seduce and impregnate young women. He lives in a dolphin paradise under the waters of the Amazon but is drawn to parties when he hears people laughing on the banks of the river. He's a great musician, loves "beautiful people," and can really dance. This legend is so commonly accepted that the Boto is listed as the father on some Amazonian birth certificates. When a young girl turns up pregnant, the conversation might go something like this:

Parents: "We are so disappointed in you! How could you do this to our family?"

Pregnant young lady: "I'm so sorry, I couldn't help it!"

Parents: "Couldn't help it! I don't need to hear this!"

Preggers" "No, no, you misunderstand! I couldn't help it, because it was the Boto."

Relieved parents: "Oh! The Boto! Nothing you could do then, of course. Your boyfriend, Murilo, seems like a nice boy. Even though it isn't his, of course, I hope maybe he will marry you and treat the child like his own? Should we plan a wedding?"

Problem. Solved. Except for Murilo, who will be raising this fishy baby for the rest of his life.

And there is the Mapinguari, the creature whose legend we were investigating. The Mapinguari is supposed to be a hero of the forest, a protector, a righter of wrongs. People have some of the best stories about this beast, each more outrageous than the last. Claws that drip with cursed blood, teeth that shred flesh, venom that makes you impotent, a stare that makes you impotent, a scream that acts like Viagra – these are truly attributes that I heard, first hand, from people throughout Amazonia and Rhodonia – and the stories just get better and better.

We were in a fish market in Parintins filming some of the locals' take on these creatures. Parintins is a community that is serious about its folklore. Their Folklore Festival (Festival Folclórico de Parintins) is the second largest party in Brazil, Carnival in Rio being the only one to draw more revelers.

Also called Boi-Bumbá, the celebration takes place over the course of three crazy days and nights in late June. The festival celebrates a local legend about a resurrected ox. It's a bit confusing and the history is murky, but it's something along the lines of the following.

A pregnant woman had a huge craving for ox tongue and her husband, a young farmhand, would do anything to satisfy her. (As a man whose wife had some odd food cravings while pregnant, I can relate to the guy.) Unfortunately for him, getting some ox tongue meant killing a very popular cow that danced for the villagers and made them laugh. They were very sad when they found out he had killed it and called the local priest to resurrect it. The priest said he couldn't do it alone, but if the whole village partied and feasted and brought enough happiness into the world, the ox would rise. Sure enough, after a three-day rager, Brazil-style, the ox came back.

A party was thrown in honor of the ox each year, which the village used as a way to teach people how the community was important, and how one person's cravings shouldn't take happiness away from others, and all kinds of feel-good commune, hippie stuff. But, as we are humans, and humans can only take so much hippie stuff, over the years a competition arose as to who could party the hardest. Yes, Brazil has a competition for the best partier.

In Parintins, the disputes were known to cause fights, and even deaths. In an effort to curb the violence, the church proposed a "healthy" competition of massive partying in 1965. They divided the town into two teams: Garantido (Red) and Caprichoso (Blue), and asked them to reenact the story of the zombie-ox. They were told to each put their own spin on it, and the assembled crowd would vote for the best performance and best party. Every year since, each team attempts to outdo the other with scantily clad dancers, elaborate musical numbers, and massive parade floats in the images of the pantheon of the mythical creatures mentioned above, and other characters from the cadre of Brazilian lore woven into the now extremely elaborate tale of the bull and a pregnant woman's appetite.

The entire town is separated by their support of Garantido or Caprichoso. In Boston, we think of the Yankees and Red Sox as a rivalry, Wales has Cardiff versus Swansea, the Ramones have Johnny or Joey fans, and Twilight has Team Jacob and Team Stalker – all of these pale in comparison to the Red/Blue rivalry of Parintins. The houses are painted red or blue, street signs are red or blue, storefronts are red or blue, cafes are divided into red and blue sections – even Coca-Cola is sold in traditional red or blue cans, and Coke promos around the city are in red or blue. Luckily, it is a friendly rivalry for the most part; after all, it is all about the best party. Incidentally, I was accepted into team Red and given a pair of knock-off white Havaianas with red hearts and bulls on them. I wear them proudly to this day.

We had already gotten more footage than we could possibly use, but the stories were so good we kept shooting. We found this one incredibly photogenic old woman working at a blue produce stand in the far corner of the market. Cinematically, it was perfect. Diffused light, exotic fruits and veggies piled around her, her heavily lined face looking the perfect mix of intimidating and trustworthy – we had to talk to her.

She was bagging little bundles of small peppers, her age-spotted fingers deftly tying knots in a well-practiced motion when we approached her. She smiled, kindly, as I started to introduce myself and the crew. She asked very politely what she could do to help us. I asked if she had ever heard of the Mapinguari and she blessed herself, held her hands to the heavens, and started rocking. Oh yeah – cameras on, we've got a live one.

"Have I heard of the Mapinguari? Jesus, yes! Jesus! Don't say the name of the beast! It is the name of the *devil*! The *evil*! The *wickedness*! It punishes all those who cross it! Don't seek this creature, young man. Leave it be! Don't look for it or you will be cursed. *Cursed!*"

Oh, this was TV gold.

"So, why is this creature so bad?" I asked, trying to sound naïve. "What does it do?"

"What does it *do*? What does it *do*? It kills! With a glance! It has one huge and terrible eye. It's the eye of the devil himself! It is filled with hate! Its mouth is filled with crooked, jagged teeth, and the blood, the blood is filled with venom and acid! The venom and acid will kill you if you touch them! Oh Jesus! Its mouth is in its chest, and its breath will choke the life out of you! And its mouth is also filled with bees! Bees that are filled with venom, and poison! Bees that will kill you!"

She kept going from there. She was really into it, and we let her go for about 15 minutes. When she was done with her warning, we thanked her and she warned us again not to search for the evil creature. I shook her hand and told her not to worry, we were trained professionals. As we walked away I turned to James and said, "Wow, this thing sounds pretty nasty." "Yeah," he replied. "It was the bees that really got me." And we both smiled.

I did my best imitation of her gravely elder-villager-in-a-horror-movie voice "Don't seek the beast! Its mouth is filled with razor sharp claws! And blood! And the blood is filled with poison. And hate!"

"And its eye makes you impotent!" chimed in Sol, in a far better impression of the woman's voice.

"And its scream sounds like a Justin Bieber song and it will make you deaf and criminally insane if you hear it!" joined in Ben.

"And its fur is on fire! And the fire will melt your eyes if you look into it!" added Brendan.

"And in the fire, there are bees! And the bees are on fire! And they will sting you! And the bees are filled with herpes!"

chimed in James.

"And you will get herpes from the bees! And chlamydia! And you'll be on fire! And your eyes will be melted! And your genitalia will fall off!" I finished.

We were all laughing hysterically by this point.

"Herpes bees," said Ben. "Yeah, maybe we shouldn't look for this thing. I don't like the sound of herpes bees, that are on fire."

But look for it we did. And we found more incredible stories. After talking to dozens of locals we found a man in a remote village on the edge of the wilderness who claimed to have seen the creature about five years previous to our meeting him – he did not mention bees or flaming fur. He was a very earnest man – probably in his late fifties. He was in good shape, despite having a bit of a pot belly. He was a farmer and saw the creature on the edge of his field one night, or so he thought.

The further into his story that he got, the more concerned we became that it was an entirely different form of mistaken identity that had taken place, which almost led to a capital crime.

He told me he heard a strange noise, like a large beast walking through his crops. He grabbed his shotgun and went to investigate. What he saw he claimed he would never forget, and the thought of it would haunt him forever. I was intrigued, and wanted to know more.

"What did the creature look like?" I asked.

"Oh, it was very big. *Very* big. Taaaaaall. It was on two legs."

"How tall?" I asked, holding my hands up to gesture around 8 feet. "Taller than this?"

"Oh no, not taller than that. Maybe a bit taller than you. Maybe two or three inches taller than you. *Very* tall, very big."

"Okay," I'm thinking, 6'2", 6'3" – that isn't that tall. But as I looked around, the tribe was all very small. The tallest person I saw around was maybe 5'5", – so, okay, 6'3" can seem kind of tall to a group of shorter people.

"So, it was a little taller than me. Was it wide? Muscular?"

"Very muscular, very strong, but not wide. Shoulders, like yours. But strong."

Okay, ouch, but moving past that. "What else can you tell me about it? Did it have claws? Could you see its face?"

"Well, it was dark. It was dark out, and the creature was dark. It had long arms. Its hair was very dark. It had a lot of hair on its arms, legs, and head. Very dark hair. I couldn't see its face."

Hair. He definitely said hair. I asked Sol, who was translating, to confirm – she conferred with him. "Yes," she said. "He believes it was hair, but very curly and thick – not like hair they have here."

Again, I looked around – this tribe had thick, straight hair on their heads, but little to no body hair. I looked at James who was open-mouthed, clearly thinking the same thing as me.

I continued questioning him. "What else can you tell me about the, um, creature?"

"It moved very hesitantly, like it was sneaking. And it had very big feet, big like yours," and he motioned to my size 10.5 boots. "Very big feet," he said again. "I yelled 'Hey! Hey! What are you doing in my field?' and it stopped. I yelled again and waved my gun and it yelled back, but I couldn't understand it. It made weird noises! Weird sounds! Like it was talking, but scary talking, and I know you aren't supposed to listen to the Mapinguari, it's bad luck, so I yelled again 'Hey! Hey! I will shoot you!', and it couldn't understand me but I was so scared! I knew it was the Mapinguari because it was so tall and so dark. Its hair was so weird! So I shot at it and it screamed! It screamed and ran away and I think I hit its arm, grazed it, or it cut itself running away because I saw little drops of blood where it had been, but I knew not to touch the blood of the Mapinguari and I was so afraid that it would come back that I told my family we had to move. So we did, we packed up that night and left, and came here."

I stood there, mouth hanging open. Clearly, he believed I was impressed and sufficiently freaked out by his terrifying encounter. And I was, but not for the reasons he thought. I looked at Ben, who looked equally as shocked. James was wide-eyed, trying to suppress a laugh as he took in all of our expressions. Sol was just shaking her head and consulting her notes. Brendan looked dumbstruck. I said, slowly, the only thing that came to mind, "I, think, you may have shot a man."

James lost it with a single barking laugh. "I'm pretty sure you shot a guy who accidently wandered into your fields and didn't speak your language." Turning away from the man whom I'd just accused of attempted murder, I said "Ben – I'm pretty sure he shot a guy. What do we do here?"

"Yup," said Ben. "There is no way we're using this footage. Sol, do you have the phone number for the local police? Let's wrap up, I think we're done here."

Acknowledgements

While I have dedicated this book to Luna and Wally (my father was quick to point out the inappropriateness of this, noting some of the adult content, and the fact that they won't be able to read for a few years), and genuinely, the greatest part of my life is being a part of theirs, but I truly could not have completed it without the help of the many incredible people I am so fortunate to have in my life. I'd like to take a minute to thank each of them.

Anna – my phenomenal wife. She not only joins me on many adventures, but has put up with all of the insanity that comes with being a partner to a guy who does all of the stuff described in here.

My insane and wonderful family – Al, Mom, Sarah, and Nathan who have supported and encouraged me throughout my life. Mom, who learned more about alligator reproduction than she probably ever wanted to in her quest to support a budding young biologist and Al who took me camping and fishing despite having no interest in these activities himself, which I never knew until I was in my late twenties. Sorry about child welfare having to come to the house and watch you change diapers and question Sarah about possible neglect/abuse after I got salmonella from a lizard, then spread it to about a dozen friends, and cracked my head open sledding, and sliced my legs open sliding down a hill to catch a snake – hopefully this makes up for the embarrassment?

The entire current and past Icon family, particularly Harry and Laura Marshall. Harry and Laura are two of my favorite people on Earth. They are the people Anna and I want to be when we grow up. They are the smartest, nicest, funniest, and most caring and loving people you could hope to meet, and the greatest thing about doing TV has been having them enter our lives. We love them like family. In addition to Harry and Laura there's Andie Clare, Lucy Middleboe, Stephen McQuillan, Barny Revill, James Bickersteth, Alex Holden, Anna Gol, Ben Roy, Laura Coates, Sol Welch, Belinda Partridge, Abi Wrigley, Duncan Fairs, Robin Cox, Simon Reay, Brendan McGinty, and everyone else, who continue to be amazing forces of encouragement and support.

The Nat Geo team behind *Beast Hunter* –

Janet Han Vissering, Steve Burns, Ashley Hoppin, Sydney Suissa, Russel Howard, Chris Albert, Geoff Daniels, Mike Mavretic, Dara Klatt, Steve Ashworth, Whit Higgins, and others. Thank you so much for your support and trust in allowing me to fulfill a lifelong dream, and letting Icon take the lead and make a series we are all really proud of.

The most amazing and supportive group of friends I could ask for – Adam Manning, Dom Pellegrino, Joe Viola, and Adrianna Wooden. Thank you for sticking by me and being there for me and my family through everything.

Thank you so much to the entire team at John Hunt Publishing, especially John Hunt, who saw the potential of the massive and messy manuscript I sent over, Dominic James, who assured all of my insecurities and answered all of my questions while reassuring me that it was all going to be okay, and the expert editing of Graham Clarke, who managed to pull these six books together and make them the cohesive series.

My very literary friends and family who served as the first reviewers of this book – Al Spain, Joe Viola, Dom Pellegrino, Richard Sugg, Sarah Franchi, Gene Campbell, Tim Fogarty, John Johnson, Zeb Schobernd, Sarahbeth Golden, and Luke Kirkland – thank you for your insights and mocking. This book is much better because of you.

The folks at my day job who have supported my insane extracurricular activities – especially Bill O'Connor who gave me the opportunity to do this and assured me I'd still have a job when I returned.

Thanks to all of the incredible fixers, guides, and translators who kept us alive and safe, often risking your own lives in the process.

Thanks, finally, to the readers and fans of these shows! I hope you've enjoyed what you've seen and read! You can find all of my social media stuff at www.patspain.com. I try to answer questions and respond as best I can. Genuinely – thank you!

Continue the adventure with the Pat Spain On the Hunt Series

A Little Bigfoot: On the Hunt in Sumatra
Pat Spain lost a layer of skin, pulled leeches off his neither regions and was violated by an Orangutan for this book
Paperback: 978-1-78904-605-2
ebook: 978-1-78904-606-9

200,000 Snakes: On the Hunt in Manitoba
Pat Spain got and lost his dream job, survived stage 3 cancer, and laid down in a pit of 200,000 snakes for this book.
Paperback: 978-1-78904-648-9
ebook: 978-1-78904-649-6

A Living Dinosaur: On the Hunt in West Africa
Pat Spain was nearly thrown in a Cameroonian prison, learned to use a long-drop toilet while a village of pygmy children watched, and was deemed "too dirty to fly" for this book.
Paperback: 978-1-78904-656-4
ebook: 978-1-78904-657-1

A Bulletproof Ground Sloth: On the Hunt in Brazil
Pat Spain participated in the most extreme tribal ritual, accidentally smuggled weapons, and almost lost his mind in the Amazonian rainforest for this book.
Paperback: 978-1-78904-652-6
ebook: 978-1-78904-653-3

The Mongolian Death Worm: On the Hunt in the Gobi Desert
Pat Spain ingested toxic "foods", made a name for himself in traditional Mongolian wrestling, and experienced the worst bathroom on Earth for this book.
Paperback: 978-1-78904-650-2
ebook: 978-1-78904-651-9

Sea Serpents: On the Hunt in British Columbia
Pat Spain went to the bottom of the ocean, triggered a bunch of
very angry fisherman, and attempted to recreate an iconic scene
from Apocalypse Now for this book.
Paperback: 978-1-78904-654-0
ebook: 978-1-78904-655-7

**6TH
BOOKS**

ALL THINGS PARANORMAL

Investigations, explanations and deliberations on the paranormal,
supernatural, explainable or unexplainable. 6th Books seeks to
give answers while nourishing the soul: whether making use of the
scientific model or anecdotal and fun, but always
beautifully written.
Titles cover everything within parapsychology: how to, lifestyles,
alternative medicine, beliefs, myths and theories.
If you have enjoyed this book, why not tell other readers by
posting a review on your preferred book site?

Recent bestsellers from 6th Books are:

The Afterlife Unveiled
What the Dead Are Telling us About Their World!
Stafford Betty
What happens after we die? Spirits speaking through mediums
know, and they want us to know. This book unveils their world...
Paperback: 978-1-84694-496-3 ebook: 978-1-84694-926-5

Spirit Release
Sue Allen
A guide to psychic attack, curses, witchcraft, spirit attachment,
possession, soul retrieval, haunting, deliverance, exorcism and
more, as taught at the College of Psychic Studies.
Paperback: 978-1-84694-033-0 ebook: 978-1-84694-651-6

I'm Still With You
True Stories of Healing Grief Through Spirit Communication
Carole J. Obley
A series of after-death spirit communications which uplift, comfort
and heal, and show how love helps us grieve.
Paperback: 978-1-84694-107-8 ebook: 978-1-84694-639-4

Less Incomplete
A Guide to Experiencing the Human Condition Beyond the
Physical Body
Sandie Gustus
Based on 40 years of scientific research, this book is a dynamic
guide to understanding life beyond the physical body.
Paperback: 978-1-84694-351-5 ebook: 978-1-84694-892-3

Advanced Psychic Development
Becky Walsh
Learn how to practise as a professional, contemporary spiritual medium.
Paperback: 978-1-84694-062-0 ebook: 978-1-78099-941-8

Astral Projection Made Easy
and overcoming the fear of death
Stephanie June Sorrell
From the popular Made Easy series, *Astral Projection Made Easy* helps to eliminate the fear of death, through discussion of life beyond the physical body.
Paperback: 978-1-84694-611-0 ebook: 978-1-78099-225-9

The Miracle Workers Handbook
Seven Levels of Power and Manifestation of the Virgin Mary
Sherrie Dillard
Learn how to invoke the Virgin Mary's presence, communicate with her, receive her grace and miracles and become a miracle worker.
Paperback: 978-1-84694-920-3 ebook: 978-1-84694-921-0

Divine Guidance
The Answers You Need to Make Miracles
Stephanie J. King
Ask any question and the answer will be presented, like a direct line to higher realms... *Divine Guidance* helps you to regain control over your own journey through life.
Paperback: 978-1-78099-794-0 ebook: 978-1-78099-793-3

The End of Death
How Near-Death Experiences Prove the Afterlife
Admir Serrano
A compelling examination of the phenomena of Near-Death
Experiences.
Paperback: 978-1-78279-233-8 ebook: 978-1-78279-232-1

Where After
Mariel Forde Clarke
A journey that will compel readers to view life after death in a
completely different way.
Paperback: 978-1-78904-617-5 ebook: 978-1-78904-618-2

Harvest: The True Story of Alien Abduction
G L Davies
G. L. Davies's most terrifying investigation yet reveals one
woman's terrifying ordeal of alien visitation, nightmarish visions
and a prophecy of destruction on a scale never before seen in
Pembrokeshire's peaceful history.
Paperback: 978-1-78904-385-3 ebook: 978-1-78904-386-0

The Scars of Eden
Paul Wallis
How do we distinguish between our ancestors' ideas of God and
close encounters of an extra-terrestrial kind?
Paperback: 978-1-78904-852-0 ebook: 978-1-78904-853-7

Readers of ebooks can buy or view any of these bestsellers by clicking on the live link in the title. Most titles are published in paperback and as an ebook. Paperbacks are available in traditional bookshops. Both print and ebook formats are available online.
Find more titles and sign up to our readers' newsletter at http://www.johnhuntpublishing.com/mind-body-spirit.
Follow us on Facebook at https://www.facebook.com/OBooks and Twitter at https://twitter.com/obooks.